Elk Hunting in the Northern Rockies

By Ed Wolff

Published in the United States of America

Elk Hunting in the Northern Rockies

By Ed Wolff

Copyright 1984 by Ed Wolff

Library of Congress Catalog Number 84-50960

ISBN 0-912299-17-7

Table of Contents

Cover Photo

Ed Wolff caught this magnificent bull in the rut with Nikon FM camera from a distance of about 35 feet. The bull had completely demolished a group of lodgepole in a matter of 10 minutes and is the process of "stinking up" a tree by rubbing it with his pre-orbital scent gland.

Dedication

This book is dedicated to the elk. Long may they roam free and wild.

Introduction

My motives for writing this book are simple. First, I personally love elk. Seeing, tracking, photographing and harvesting them bring me hours of enjoyment. The elk, indeed, is one of the world's premiere big game animals. Second, the Northern Rockies region has numbers of good — no, excellent — elk hunters. Many have fascinating stories to tell, some of which I personally have had the pleasure of hearing. Often these were told around a campfire in a special place — a secret site known only to a few close friends. My purpose for writing this book is to help you understand the species characteristics of elk and to share the five great hunting tales.

I hope you glean a few useful facts from this book. Putting it together gave me the opportunity to rub elbows with some mighty fine people. I have a feeling that I'm the recipient of the greatest benefit of its production.

The original format I chose for this book was to present two sections. The first part would be devoted to discussing elk and their species characteristics. The second part would relate five elk hunting tales as told by, in their own words, some of the most knowledgeable, successful elk hunters I could find. The first portion flowed much as planned, but the second section, I soon discovered, could not stop at simply telling the stories. It would have been incomplete. The five hunters interviewed for hunting tales are well versed in elk hunting techniques and also know a great deal about elk as a species. All were exciting to listen to; they often diverged away from their hunting stories to relate some gem of wisdom. Not wanting to omit these "gems," I added a question and answer section after each hunter's story.

Each individual freely shared his wealth of knowledge concerning the art of elk hunting. This experience has been gained by spending many hours and years not only hunting elk, but observing them during the off-season. Each hunter also has a keen feeling for the well-being and preservation of elk, and it has been a privilege to preserve their stories and share them with you. I will be forever grateful for their patience and assistance, without which these pages would have never seen the light of day. I'm richer for the experience. I hope that this book will also enrich the mystique of the elk species.

I solicit you to read and re-read carefully the five chapters involving them, not only to enjoy again the hunting adventures but to read between the lines to learn and polish your skills. Each author uses a different approach to elk hunting and, frankly, I was surprised at the lack of uniformity in their techniques.

One final word. If you want to hunt elk, don't wait. Do it now! Enjoy the magnificent Northern Rocky Mountain back country this fall. The land is waiting and there just might be a big bull with your name on him. I suspect, though, that your greatest reward will come from the hunt. Harvesting an elk isn't always the highlight of the trip.

My special thanks to Kathy Rehbein, who very patiently molded masses of incoherent sentences and paragraphs into a palatable reading form. Thank you Kathy. Thanks also to my good friends, John Wozniak, who reviewed this manuscript, and to Gary Holmes, who opened his slide files to me. Many of Gary's excellent images appear in these pages.

Ed Wolff
Missoula, Montana
May, 1984

Elk Hunting in the Northern Rockies

In my opinion there is one sound that typifies wildness, a sound that stirs contemporary man's primitive instincts and makes an outdoor experience rich. It is the deep, gutteral roar of a herd bull elk rising from the dark of a north-facing lodgepole jungle. Clear and crisp the sound spills from deep within the bull's chest and carries through the frosty pre-dawn air. Other natural sounds, like the honking of a wedge of high-flying geese, also stir the imagination — but nothing does it quite like a shrill bugle of a rutting bull elk.

The Northern Rockies is an exciting place to be in the fall. The dog days of August have passed, exchanged for cool, invigorating days and frosty nights. The seasons are changing and the hunter feels it in the atmosphere. The air becomes electric! Elk feel the change, too. In the wild, large, mature bulls seek out and gather harems of cows, while hunters tend to the final details of organizing their trips in quest of those elk.

Elk hunting is not just for one type of person. It is for all those who appreciate a wilderness experience, enjoy hearing and seeing elk, get excited at following elk tracks or squeezing elk manure, or who simply want to harvest a trophy or meat. Serious elk hunters are consumed with thoughts of high alpine meadows laced with timbered draws, horse sweat, the feel of old leather, comradeship, and, of course, the clear whine of the bull elk of their dreams just up ahead on the next ridge.

Because elk live in diverse habitats, there are many different methods of hunting them. Therefore, a hunter can tailor an elk hunt to suit his or her specific needs and desires. Hunting elk can be intensely serious business or it can be approached in a more relaxed manner. Because elk are so noble a creature and their habitat so pristine, it is best to think of hunting them as a total wilderness experience with the harvesting of an elk not necessarily the ultimate criteria of success. A strong case can be made for the emotional and spiritual satisfaction one derives from sharing a wild Rocky Mountain basin with a close friend, or with one's own private thoughts. However, the ultimate test of one's skill, mental discipline and physical condition can be experienced hunting the lone herd bulls back in the high country late in November. It is a supreme test of one-on-one and, at the same time, a highly rewarding experience.

On the other end of the spectrum is the guided hunt provided by an experienced outfitter. Accommodations are furnished as well as guides who are familiar with the country and the species. And let's face it, because of demands on a person's time and geographical distribution of our population, a guided elk hunt is the only opportunity many hunters will ever have to enjoy the experience of seeing an elk track in the mud, let alone hunting elk.

Either method and all phases in between, with a few exceptions, can be equally fulfilling ways of taking elk. It is all in the mind of the doer.

Elk live in diverse habitats even within the confines of the Northern Rockies, giving the novice or experienced hunter a variety of habitat types to hunt. The Wind River country of Wyoming, for instance, contains some of the most spectacular back country in North America. Many peaks over 12,000 feet crown the isolated, timbered drainages. The country is truly wild and offers a not-to-be-forgotten wilderness hunt.

Montana offers, perhaps, the most diversified elk habitat although its mountains rarely exceed 10,000 feet in altitude. The northwest section of the state holds an almost jungle-like environment of dense evergreens covering an understory of thick brush. The west-central section holds high, rugged mountains as well as timbered lower country sprinkled with open, south-facing parks. Montana even offers limited elk hunting in a prairie or "breaks" environment.

Idaho's prime elk habitat is much like west and west-central Montana's. However, the mountains of the Salmon River Breaks are very steep, primitive, and dominating — offering a unique type of hunt.

As one would suspect, elk, because of their diverse habitat types and wide distribution, can be hunted by a variety of styles.

Historically elk existed primarily as a plains animal and early explorers reported seeing great herds of them.

In realty, almost every died-in-the-wool elk hunter has developed techniques and quirks of his or her own. None are necessarily wrong. It's just that there are a lot of methods used to solve the elk hunting riddle.

A few hardy hunters prefer to hunt elk alone under the harshest of conditions where the hunter's survival can be a problem. They want the challenge. Others prefer to hunt the mature, herd type bulls during the rut. Bugling and grunting elk is their game, which is further complicated because they hunt with a bow. Stealth and deception are their methods.

Some elk hunters cover vast amounts of country during the hunting day. Talus slides and thick timber are no obstacle while covering 12 to 15 miles per day looking for elk concentrations. They are like hounds on a scent. Other individuals prefer a more relaxed state of affairs and hunt with a group of friends. Their main objective is camaraderie and escapism. Killing an elk is important, but not mandatory to a happy hunt.

Hunters in general tend to settle into whatever style of elk hunting they are comfortable with — a style they succeed with, though often "success" is defined only in the mind of the individual.

I've discovered one common characteristic for those who measure success by the harvesting of an elk year after year, and

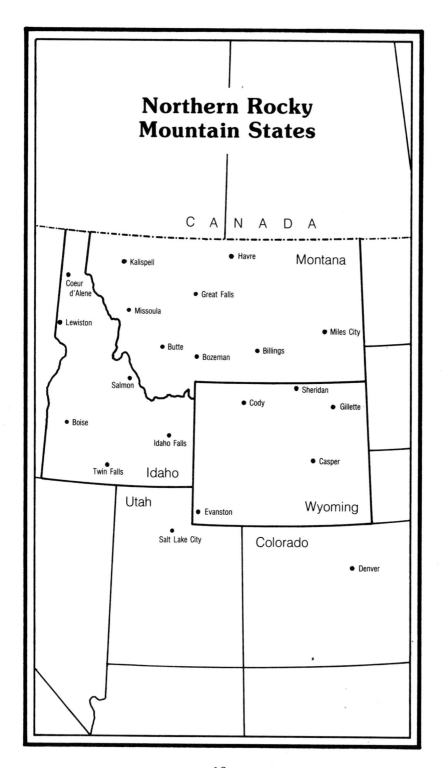

Northern Rocky Mountain States

C A N A D A

Montana

- Kalispell
- Havre
- Great Falls
- Missoula

Coeur
d'Alene

- Lewiston

- Miles City

- Butte
- Billings
- Bozeman

Salmon

- Sheridan
- Cody
- Gillette

- Boise

- Idaho Falls

- Casper

Twin Falls

Idaho

- Evanston

Wyoming

Utah

Salt Lake City

Colorado

- Denver

that is persistence. Hunting often, long and hard is the key.

The truly nice thought about elk is that they can be enjoyed in so many different ways. They can be hunted in a serious or a carefree manner. Immense pleasure also is found in observing and photographing elk in Yellowstone or Glacier National Parks, or in the wild for that matter. Studying elk in their natural environment, their tracks, rubs, and wallows provides hours of enjoyment. One learns that it's just good to know that elk are around, free and wild.

In the Northern Rockies, much of the elk hunting is done on public land. In Montana, 80 percent of the harvested elk are taken on those public lands. This is land that every American owns and has a right to use in a responsible manner. For the most part, these lands are devoid of fences and no-trespassing signs. It is an exciting prospect to realize that we as citizens of the United States have free, unlimited access to millions of acres of national forests and wilderness areas. We can enjoy the breathtaking scenery and use the bountiful game.

The United States was one of the earliest countries to recognize by law that its game species are owned by the state rather than individuals. This holds true whether the land on which the game is found is public or private. America's wildlife resource is community property to be managed by state fish and game departments, the Bureau of Land Management, the U.S. Forest Service, and the U.S. Fish and Wildlife Service.

In the period following the mass slaughter of wild ungulates in North America (1900-1950), game management programs were established by state and federal agencies to enable the wildlife to recover. The dual need of expanding their numbers and extending their range were met.

Hunting was recognized as an indispensable element of game management since the wolf and the mountain lion, elk's natural predators, had become nearly extinct. However, inaccessibility to many elk strongholds caused herd populations to mushroom, overburdening the carrying capacity of the range. In the Rockies, between 1950 and 1960, elk hunting regulations were liberalized to take care of the overpopulation problem. Seasons in some regions were up to two months long and open to the taking of either bull or cow elk.

This all changed in the 1960s as logging roads were punched into formerly virgin country. Roads gave hunters access to large areas of backcountry, while logging of immense tracts of land reduced the amount of escape cover. Between 1970 and 1980, timber harvests increased threefold and elk populations plummeted. Harvest regulations were again tightened.

In Montana between 1960 and 1970, hunting seasons lasted

The spine-tingling bugle of a herd bull signals his dominance.

about 35 days. However, the right to hunt elk of either-sex on a non-permit basis was reduced by 28 percent, with a further reduction by 84 percent during 1970-1980. Since 1980, cow elk may be taken only with a special permit. There is no non-permit, either-sex elk hunting during the general season. Tightening of elk hunting regulations is due primarily to the impact of habitat reduction and not because of the increase in the number of hunters — even though the number of hunters increased from 60,000 in 1960 to 90,000 in 1982. The percentage of successful hunters has remained in the 12 percent to 14 percent range for the past several seasons. There is, of course, the intangible effect of increased harassment of elk brought about the more hunters in the woods.

The largest elk harvests in the United States during 1979 were in Colorado and Wyoming, where more than 27,800 and nearly 18,600 legal elk were bagged, respectively.[7] Harvest can fluctuate in any state from year to year, due to a variety of factors such as weather during the hunting season, hunter numbers, and elk populations. Montana's elk harvest has not varied much from an annual kill of 10,000 to 14,000 animals during the past 20 years. In 1981, however, the kill slipped a little to 13,055 animals, down about 8 percent from 1980. In Idaho, the elk harvest has shown a sharp drop since 1968 to a level of near 6,000 animals in 1979. This has been blamed on degenerating habitat. In 1981, there were 9,903 elk taken in Idaho, representing a 20 percent gain from 1980.

Today's sportsman hunts mainly for recreation with the harvesting of meat being of secondary importance, although the challenge of nature coupled with the chance to bag a trophy or bring home a piece of meat are motivators for many. Hunting becomes a yearly ritual that sees hunters returning to the same woods with similar hunting companions sharing campfires and outdoor experiences.

Roughly 10.5 million people hunt big game in the United States. Man, after all, has been a predator and hunter for millenium. The hunting urge is ingrained deeply in our genetic makeup. Modern man, however, as a harvester of big game has an individual obligation to respect and protect our wildlife resources and the habitats in which they live. This obligation, since hunting is a solo sport or accomplished with a few close friends, is self imposed. Hunting's moral conduct is policed by each individual's conscience.

Hunting quality, number of elk seen, and the number of days spent afield are factors of concern and importance to today's sportsman. Hunter success as measured by the amount of game bagged is no longer valid. Sighting, stalking, and outwitting elk in

A Guide to Hunting Regulations and Fees

IDAHO

The early season begins Sept. 15, with late seasons running through Nov. 21. A nonresident license costs $75.50 plus $150.50 for an elk tag. Nonresident tags are limited to 9,500, with 1,200 specified for the Panhandle Region in northern Idaho and 8,300 for the remainder of the state. Elk tags sell out in the Panhandle, but the others don't — probably because access to the rest of the elk country is difficult. Contact the Idaho Fish and Game Department, 600 South Walnut, Box 25, Boise, ID 83707; Phone 208-334-3700.

MONTANA

The general season begins Sept. 4 for bowhunters. Gun hunters can get into the Bob Marshall Wilderness and southcentral areas beginning Sept. 15. The general hunt usually extends from the last week of October through the Thanksgiving Day weekend. The nonresident license fee is $300. Deer, bear, elk, birds, and fish may be taken with that license. There are 17,000 nonresident permits allotted on a first-come, first-serve basis and they go quickly. In 1984, all 17,000 were gone within three weeks of their availability. Contact the Montana Department of Fish, Wildlife and Parks, 1420 East Sixth St., Helena, MT 59620; Phone 406-444-2535.

WYOMING

The earliest rifle hunt is Sept. 10, followed by openings on Oct. 1 and Nov. 1. A nonresident license fee is $255 and the deadline for an elk application is Feb. 1. About 6,000 permits are issued for nonresidents but the department emphasizes that these regulations are subject to change at any time. Contact the Wyoming Fish and Game Department, Cheyenne, Wyoming 82002; Phone 307-777-7631.

their home environment is becoming more important to sportsmen and the actual kill is anticlimatic to many hunters — as demonstrated by the steady growth of archery hunting. The woodsman's skills have to be honed to a higher degree by the archer than the rifleman.

Professional wildlife managers manipulate the environment and manage game populations so the animals themselves can prosper from the harvest and sportsmen can enjoy a quality hunting adventure. In today's world, these are difficult objectives to obtain. Numerous interests pull at the land and compete for its use.

Other recreational activities must be considered, too, such as cross-country skiing, backpacking, snowmobiling, and the nonhunting enjoyment of elk. The best balance allows the largest number of people to gain the most benefit, with no one group applying too much pressure on the elk population or its habitat.

Hunting regulations and laws are major techniques used to control the elk harvest. Seasons, bag limits, and specific areas made open to hunters are determined after considering input from state fish and game departments, wildlife biologists, landowners, and survey information obtained from hunters. Hunting regulations are subject to frequent and sometimes sudden changes in response to the needs of the habitat or elk populations.

Timing of the hunting seasons varies from year to year and state to state. Some states have an archery season preceding the general season. General seasons are open to the public and only the purchase of a license is necessary to hunt. This system permits the individual a wide variety of places to hunt, but often only bull elk can be taken.

Some states have special hunts. For instance, Montana has a long late-season hunt in the areas adjacent to Yellowstone Park. It runs during the months of December, January and February and is designed to control the size of the park herd.

Managed or controlled hunts may be held in a certain area with a specific problem in order to harvest a set number of elk. These kind of regulations are designed to bring an elk population back into balance with respect to the number or type of elk in a specific herd or area.

A trophy bull elk with antler beams of more than five feet is difficult to come by these days. While most elk hunters express a desire to harvest a trophy bull, the majority settle for the first legal elk that affords a shot. The fact is that bulls possessing trophy antlers are mature, older bulls. These bulls must have sufficient, remote habitat to reach the age of 7 to 10 years.

To reach trophy size, an elk must have habitat with the proper

Open parks associated with heavy timber offer optimum elk habitat.

amounts and quality of forage. Additionally, state game departments must direct management programs toward the production of trophy bulls. One method of accomplishing this is to carry the largest number of elk necessary to produce superior bulls. Large populations of elk result in a higher number of bulls, with each bull having less chance of being killed during the hunting season. Unfortunately, game management agencies do not manage elk populations for the production of trophies. The net result is that mature trophy bulls are becoming scarce, while 2- and 3-year-old bulls are harvested in greater numbers.

Montana has one notable exception that allows it to produce more "book heads" than any other state. It is the late, mid-winter hunt that takes place in the country immediately bordering Yellowstone National Park. This hunt offers a good chance to harvest a big bull.

The location and timing of the hunt bring together a unique set of circumstances. Yellowstone Park provides an environment for bulls to grow to a ripe, old age and also contains vast, open parks with highly-nutritious forage. Also, the Yellowstone Plateau is at a high elevation and, during the hunting period, has deep snow and bitter cold. Therefore, the big bulls are forced down to accessible elevations outside the park. Further, the snow can be so deep that it severely restricts the elk's movements. This further enhances the hunter success rate, which borders on 90 percent plus.

I'm not implying that trophy bulls cannot be found in other areas of Montana or in the other Northern Rocky Mountain states. Large, antlered bulls are present in every herd, but they are elusive and hard to locate. Hunts held during the rutting season, when bulls can be responsive to the bugle, may offer the best opportunity for the hunter to be selective and possibly lure in a sizable bull.

What it's all about — a bull elk surprised by an intruder in his lodgepole pine haven glares at a hunter at extremely close range. This is a fine trophy bull.

The History of Elk Hunting

The original range of American elk extended across the North American continent and included the entire Rocky Mountain region. It was the most widely distributed deer.

The Rocky Mountain elk originally were animals of the plains, congregating in wooded bottomlands, brushy ravines, and river breaks. In Montana, they existed in great herds in the eastern and central parts of the state, away from the mountainous regions of the west-central and north. The mountains of Idaho, likewise, had limited populations of elk. The journals of Lewis and Clark report large numbers of elk, bison, grizzlies and antelope on the plains of what is now Montana. Beyond the mouth of the Yellowstone River toward the mountains the explorers found a region swarming with wildlife. "Great numbers of Buffalow, Elk, Deer, antilope, beaver, porcupins and water fowls were seen to-day," wrote Clark on Friday, May 1, 1805.[1]

At the advent of the 20th Century, many forces were at work destroying the seemingly limitless numbers of western plains elk. Timber barons, agricultural and livestock industries, market hunters, and man's greed for land ownership all played a part is decreasing the herds and forcing a small remnant population into isolated, inaccessible pockets high in the mountains. Being reasonably adaptable animals, the elk survived, while grizzlies and bison, their plains neighbors, all but perished as wild species.

By 1900, elk populations in North America were at an all-time

A bull elk in country typical of where they're often found today, open reaches mixed with timbered draws and good cover.

low, perhaps 50,000 to 100,000 animals. At that time elk had been removed from 90 percent of their historic range. E. T. Seaton, who authored several books in the first half of this century describing hoofed mammals in North America, estimated that as many as 10,000,000 elk existed in North America prior to the coming of European man. The largest surviving remnant population of Rocky Mountain elk centered in and around Yellowstone Park. This population served as a fountainhead for nearly all present-day herds.

Forced from the plains and bottomlands, elk began the slow process of replenishing numbers in the mountain wilderness. They learned to negotiate the high passes and locate high mountain meadows that offered food and calving areas. These fine animals continue to make a remarkable recovery.

In addition, man aided this prized trophy animal by introducing, or reintroducing, it into many areas since 1892. Between the years 1892 and 1936, 5,210 elk were shipped to 32 states. This restocking program brought good populations of elk to most of the suitable habitat in the Northern Rockies. In the late 1970s, the combined totals of all sub-species of elk in North America was approximately 500,000 animals.

Fortunately for us, a trapper named Osborne Russell trapped and hunted the Yellowstone country from 1834 to 1843, during the peak of the beaver trade. Unusual for the times, Russell was also a reasonably proficient writer and recorded many of his experiences in the wilderness that would later become Utah, Montana and Wyoming. Here are a few excerpts from his accounts, which were published in a book titled *Journal of a Trapper* :[2]

August 21, 1835: "We crossed the mountains thro a defile in a west direction and fell on to a small branch of the Gallatin. Here we encamped on a small clear spot and killed the fattest Elk I ever saw. It was a large buck the fat on his rump measured seven inches thick and he had 14 spikes or branches on the left horn and 12 on the right."

One is moved to reflect on the magnitude of such a bull. Russell routinely saw large numbers of elk and killed many for food. He was a trapper concerned mainly with trapping beaver and keeping his hair out of the hands of the Blackfeet. Yet, here is a bull elk so huge that even Russell took note of the size of its rack in his journal. It seems likely that this bull was the all-time best ever taken, with the trophy rack being left to the porcupines and weather.

January 26, 1839: "I ascended the river traveling on the ice and land alternately about 4 Ms further and encamped for the night. This was a severe cold night but I was comfortably situated with one Blanket and two Epishemores and plenty of dry wood to make a fire, when I arose in the morning I discovered a band of Elk about a half a mile up the mountain. I took my rifle and went to approach them thro the snow 3 ft deep and when within about 250 paces of them they took the wind of me and ran off leaving me to return to my encampment with the consolation that this was not the first time the wind had blown away my breakfast."

August 12, 1837: "Myself and Allen (which was the name of the backwoodsman) started to hunt the small streams in the mountains to the West of us leaving the Englishman (who was the other trapper) to set traps about the camp we hunted the branches of the stream then crossed the divide to the waters of the Yellowstone Lake where we found the whole country swarming with Elk we killed a fat Buck for supper and encamped for the night."

Russell decided against describing the various forms of wildlife he encountered during his trapping days while writing his journal in the field. Instead, he wrote a more compact description of them years later while living in Oregon, after he had given up the life of a trapper.

He said about the elk: "They are very timid and harmless even when so disabled as to render escape impossible its speed is very

The Yellowstone country at the beginning of the 20th Century held the largest remaining population of elk.

swift when running single but when running in large bands they soon become wearied by continual collision with each other and if they are closely pursued by the hunter on horseback they soon commence dropping down flat on the ground to elude their pursuers and will suffer themselves to be killed with a knife in this posture. When a band is first located the hunters keep at some distance behind to avoid dispersing them and to frighten them the more a continual noise is kept up by hallooing and shooting over them which causes immediate confusion and collision of the band and the weakest Elk soon begin to drop to the ground exhausted. Their rutting time is in Sepr. when they collect in immense bands among the timber along the streams and Mtns.

"In the month of Sepr. the males have a peculiar shrill call which commences in a piercing whistle and ends in a coarse gurgling in the throat by this they call the remales to assemble and each other to the combat in which by their long antlers they are rendered formidable to each other the hair stands erect and the head is lowered to give or receive the attack but the Victor seldom pursues the vanquished."

Wyoming has always held a larger elk population than any other state. With elk numbers dwindling within the state at the beginning of the 20th Century, however, the Wind River, Teton, and Yellowstone country became a last sanctuary. Here elk

In the early years of settlement in the West, elk were killed by the thousands by commercial hunters, who sold the hides for $2.50 to $3.50 each.

numbers persisted in the mountains until public outcry brought about recognition of their plight and subsequent protection.

Rapidly declining populations of elk and bison were 2 of the primary reasons that on March 1, 1872, the U.S. Congress passed and President Ulysses S. Grant signed into law the Yellowstone Organic Act. This farsighted act was the first piece of legislation to create a wildlife park ever, anywhere in the world. Thus was born Yellowstone National Park.

Land was to be set aside "...to provide against the wanton destruction of the fish and game..." living within its boundaries. Provisions were not made, however, to enforce the park regulations. There were no resources or authority to do so. Commercial hide and meat hunters had little difficulty maintaining their operations within the park boundaries. Their poaching nearly wiped out the bison.

A journalist from Cheyenne, Wyoming, R. E. Strahorn, made the following observation: "The only blemishes in all this exquisite workmanship of nature are chargeable to man. Hunters (he is referring to commercial hunters) have for years devoted themselves to the slaughter of game until within the limits of the park it is hardly to be found. During the winter of 1874-75 at which season the heavy snows render the elk easy prey, no less than 2,000 of these were thus destroyed within a radius of 15 miles from Mammoth Hot Springs. From this large number, the skins only were taken, netting $2.50 to $3.50 apiece, the frozen caracasses being left to feed the wolves or decay in the spring."

Park rangers in Yellowstone are currently having severe problems with poachers who kill elk to collect their antlers. Even shed antlers and the antlers of winter-killed bulls are taken. Killing of bull elk in Yellowstone Park has become a particularly acute problem during the rutting period in September when the bulls are more vulnerable. In 1983, for example, a group of photographers I was with was stopped by a ranger and questioned about gunshots occurring in the area. It was a very disturbing experience. A lucrative market for powdered antlers exists in the Orient where it is believed to be a potent aphrodisiac. Antlers in the velvet have a much greater value.

In the past, antlers brought as much as $6 per pound — with a pair from a large bull weighing as much as 50 pounds.

I had a firsthand experience with antler poachers recently in Yellowstone. Late one winter I happened upon a large bull elk that had recently died as a result of severe winter conditions. I was in the park for the specific purpose of photographing winter-killed big game and took several excellent photographs of this bull and the various "natural" sanitation crews that were quickly picking the carcass clean. I returned two and one-half months later to complete my photo sequence and, to my consternation, discovered the massive antlers gone, sawed off and removed, even though the bull had died in a remote portion of the park.

Until the mid-1890s, the commercial hide hunters and "tuskers" operated with relative ease within the boundaries of Yellowstone Park and surrounding mountains. It is reported that elk carcasses and bleached antlers could be seen on every hillside. Finally, word of the carnage trickled back East, spread by journalists and editors of the prominent periodicals of the time. Firm action was taken. Through political maneuvering and adjustments in the laws, poaching for profit was brought under control. In 1895 Wyoming had a 10-month closed season on elk hunting, one of the first such laws in the West.

When Wyoming was granted statehood in 1890, settlement of the area around Yellowstone Park increased. The area south of the park, known as Jackson Hole, was especially attractive to pioneers because of its fertile ground and adequate supplies of water. Again, the elk came out second best as livestock competed for forage, especially during the critical winter months. Additionally, ranchers killed elk to prevent damage to winter hay supplies. These problems partially were solved in 1912, when Congress established the National Elk Refuge at Jackson,

This tremendous example of the species, a bull elk with massive antlers, bugles amidst a lodgepole pine jungle where he'd gathered a sizable herd of cows.

Wyoming. The creation of the refuge provided both care and protection for the elk during the difficult winter months. By this time, as previously mentioned, elk had been eliminated from 90 percent of their historical range. The protected herds in Yellowstone Park and at the National Elk Refuge have been primary sources for elk restocking programs all across North America.

By the early 1900s, the days of the "great hunts" were over. Vast herds of ungulates (hoofed mammals) had been wiped out. Pitifully few bison remained anywhere in North America, while the elk, deer, and antelope numbers were greatly reduced. Luckily for Americans today, a few visionaries during those dark periods in our wildlife history realized that a priceless national treasure was slipping away. One of those farsighted men, Theodore Roosevelt, was in a position of power to take positive, effective action before it was too late. As 26th President of the United States, he, along with George Bird Grinnell, Bing Darling, Olaus Murie, and Aldo Leopold, to name a few of the outstanding men of the time who were concerned about preserving our nation's wildlife resource, realized the herds were exhaustible. Together they fostered the concept of wildlife conservation. They helped change America's consciousness and brought about a public awareness that conserving the nation's natural resources was prudent. Today's thriving elk herds are a tribute to them.

Roosevelt was directly responsible for setting aside millions of acres of land to conserve natural resources. He, aided by Chief Forester Gifford Pinchot, achieved an impressive list of victories. Near the end of his second term in office, millions of acres of forest land had been officially preserved for the people and the nation's wildlife. Five new national parks had been created along with 16 national monuments and 51 wildlife refuges. These lands provided places for elk, deer, antelope and bison to recover their numbers. Today, wild, free-ranging elk are found in 12 states and three provinces.

In 1908, Roosevelt told a meeting of governors: "We have admitted the right of the individual to injure the future of the republic for his own present profit. The time has come for a change. As a people we have the right and duty of obeying the moral law, of requiring and doing justice, to protect ourselves and our children against the wasteful development of our natural resources."

Roosevelt was an avid hunter who pursued his interest extensively across North America and Africa. By personal example and through legislation, he influenced the course of modern game management. Elk and bison once were killed by the tens of thousands for hides, meat and teeth. Now they are managed for a wide range of uses, both recreational and biological. Hunting elk for recreation stems from a different set of values than does market hunting. Each recreational hunter sets his own standards and ethics of the hunt. Each portion of the hunt, be it the harvest, camaraderie around the campfire, or the stalk, brings forth a separate emotional high for today's elk hunter.

REFERENCES CITED

1. SNYDER, G.S. *In the Footsteps of Lewis and Clark.* Washington, D.C., National Geographic Society, 1970, Pp. 113.
2. Russell, O., edited by Haines, A. L. *Journal of a Trapper.* Lincoln, Nebraska, Bison Books 1955. Pp. 29, 66, 94, 137, 138.
3. Tilden, F. *Following the Frontier with Jay Haynes.* New York: Alfred A. Knopf, 1964. Pp 414.
4. Gerson, N.B. *A Biographical Novel About Theodore Roosevelt.* New York. Doubleday and Co., Inc. 1970. Pp 354.

Characteristics of the Species

As with all wild animals, elk are creatures of their environment and its influences. Over thousands of years, their body structure and environmental adaptations of organ function have produced a very rugged animal. Their natural environment can indeed be harsh. Temperatures in the Northern Rockies are characterized by a wide range of fluctuations from season to season. In fact, the only thing normal about mountain weather is its abnormality. "If you don't like the current weather situation, wait a few minutes and it will change," goes the saying.

As I write this, the temperature outside my office is minus 15 degrees Fahrenheit. The wind is blowing 8 to 15 miles per hour, creating a wind chill in the neighborhood of minus 40 degrees Fahrenheit. It takes a special critter to withstand temperatures like this day after day, night after night, for weeks and sometimes months on end. Elk have, mind you, no external source of heat except an often-weak sun. Today two feet of snow surround my home, which is at 4,900 feet elevation. This greatly complicates the food gathering ability of elk, especially in the spring when the snow melts during the day and then refreezes into a hard crust during the night. Such conditions make it extremely difficult for elk to paw through the crust for grass. All this takes a toll at a time when elk are especially vulnerable. Their fat and tissue reserves are low following the long winter months. Many won't survive.

An elk's physical environment is also demanding. The animals spend the summer and fall at high elevations, frequently above 8,500 feet. The country is steep and rocky. Migration routes often take the herds through narrow passes and onto slopes choked by blown-down trees. In spite of the physical barriers, the elk thrive. All this is even more amazing when one remembers that just 80 years ago, elk primarily were plains animals.

The elk is a large ungulate. In the deer family only the moose is heavier and taller. An average-sized elk is five feet at the shoulder, with bulls weighing about 700 to 850 pounds when in their prime and cows tipping the scales at 450 to 500 pounds live weight. An especially large bull, weighed by Murie in Wyoming, was 1,032 pounds live weight, 657 dressed. Most of us will have to be content to pursue the more average-sized animal.

When discussing weight in elk, it is important to remember that it will vary a great deal with the seasons. A weight loss of 45 to 65 pounds for a mature adult elk during the winter months is not uncommon.

In winter, elk develop a dense, grey-colored undercoat. It is like wool in its properties and provides superior insulating qualities. The undercoat is overlain with guard hairs that give the elk its color. Shading and color variations in the coat are influenced by the age of the animal and the season of the year. Most elk are a brown-grey on the sides and a deep chocolate, almost black, color on the neck and legs. The rump patch, usually some shade of tan, will give an animal's presence away to the careful observer. As a bull becomes older and more mature, he will tend to be a lighter straw color.

A large, mature bull about seven or eight years old and in his prime will have a pair of antlers that is truly a magnificent sight. Their growth and development are influenced by hormones, nutrition, heredity, and the general state of health of the bull. Usually the antlers of a normal adult elk have 6 points on a main beam that sweeps up and back from the head. There is no palmation. The antlers may have several curves or undulations, giving a certain character to an individual bull.

The brow tine is the first tine to grow off the main beam near its base. Close to the brow tine and next in line is the bez tine. Both extend out and down over the muzzle and turn up at the tips. Higher up on the main beam is the trez tine, followed by the sword tine. The sword or dagger tine is often the dominant point, being very long and heavy. The remaining two points, sometimes referred to as sur royals, are smaller and appear as a fork at the end of the main beam.

The color of the antlers can vary from animal to animal depending on what the bull has been rubbing his antlers on. Various shades of dark, greyish browns to almost black-brown are seen. Younger bulls frequently have antlers that are more tan or light brown in color. The ends of the tines are snow white back a distance of about 3 to 5 inches from the tips. This results from the bull goring the ground and abrading the color. The tine tips often have scars etched in them as a result of the bull goring gravels or rocky soil.

Once, while photographing elk during the rut in Yellowstone Park, I heard the deep grunt of a good bull coming through a lodgepole thicket toward my position. The dawn light, filtered by thick trees, was dim, almost like night. Suddenly, just ahead, it looked as if a candelabra with lighted candles was being carried through the woods. It was indeed my bull, the shiny white tips of his 12 big points bobbing and glowing as he approached.

The first set of antlers usually begins to grow in late May when the bull is nearly 1 year old. This set normally is just spikes that average 12 to 20 inches in length. The second set of antlers will have a shape approximating the rack of the typical 6-point mature bull. These early antlers are thin, lacking length and mass. They have have as few as 3, or as many as 6 points.

When the bull is 3 years old and growing his third set of antlers, often 4 to 5 points will be seen on a side, although some bulls may already have all 6 points. The antlers are slightly heavier with the pedicel near the base of the antler a little thicker. Subsequent antlers normally have 6 points to a side and will continue to increase in length and mass until the bull is in his prime at 8 to 12 years of age. In his declining years the bull's antlers will degenerate, becoming shorter in beam and tine length. The majority of elk shed their antlers the last two weeks of March or the first week of April each year. New antler growth starts almost immediately.

Trophy elk are classified in three sizes, and good specimens are indeed breathtaking to anyone who appreciates elk. A "Royal" refers to a bull with 6 points on each antler. "Imperial" is the category for a bull with 7 points on each antler, while a bull with 8 points per antler is called a "Monarch."

As of 1981, the largest trophy elk ever taken and recorded was killed in Dark Canyon, Colorado, in 1899. It scored 442-3/8 Boone and Crockett points. The right main beam measured 55-5/8 inches and the left beam measured 59-5/8 inches with an inside spread of 45-5/8 inches. The rack had 8 points on the right antler and 7 points on the left antler. The circumference of the right antler between the brow and bez tine was 12-1/8 inches.

On a positive note, a number of good bulls have been taken recently in the Northern Rockies. The province of Alberta in

Weather conditions during the brutal months of December, January and February can push elk to the limits of their endurance.

Canada produced an excellent bull in the early 1980s. Montana, during the 1983 season, produced several high-scoring bulls. Trophies are still being produced, but collecting one can be a real challenge.

As with all members of the ungulate class of animals, elk are ruminants. This means elk have four stomachs which enable them to digest all types of coarse forage foods. These four stomachs, the rumen in particular, collectively act as "fermentation vats" that help the breakdown of cellulose into usable nutrients. The process is very complex and not within the scope of this book.

Because of their ability to digest a broad range of plant materials, elk are able to inhabit different types of terrain and switch from one food source to another. If, for instance, the grass forage is covered by deep snow, the elk may find it necessary to change their diet to a taller browse-type plant. Adaptability can mean the difference in their survival. Being a mixed feeder, elk can eat grasses, forbs, browse, and bark. They do, however, prefer grass-type forage if available.

The elk's ability to handle a diverse diet has been a major factor in their successful move from a plains to a mountain environment. Elk have proven to be able to maintain their reproductive potential even in marginal habitats. Surprisingly, when a choice of foods is available, elk have the capacity to choose foods that contain the optimum amounts of nutrients and those which are the most digestible.

Breeding reaches its height from September 20th to the end of the month, while June is the peak of the calving time. The gestation period then is about 8 to 8 and one-half months. Single calves are the norm. The reproductive capacity of an elk population is influenced by many factors. Population structure, or the ratio of experienced bulls to breeding cows, is important. A minimum of 3 to 10 breeding bulls per 100 mature cows is necessary to maintain a viable population. Bulls generally are 3 years old before becoming sexually active enough to contribute significantly to the genetic pool of a well-balanced population. However, spikes and young bulls will do considerable breeding in the absence of mature bulls. It has been demonstrated that calves born from spikes and young bulls tend to be born weaker and have a higher mortality rate.

Few bulls live long enough to reach the age of sexual incapacity that usually occurs beyond the age 12 years. Nutrition also plays a critical role in reproductive capacity since an undernourished elk population will have poor reproductive potential. Weak, small and poorly-developed calves will result from underweight, malnourished cows.

The ability of calves to survive their first winter depends on their maturity, severity of the winter, and the quality and availability of forage. Predation is another cause of calf losses. Coyotes and black bears are the two most important predators of elk calves. In recent years, losses of calves to black bears has been particularly heavy in north-central Idaho. Up to 50 percent loss has been reported.

When calves reach the age of two to three weeks and the bands begin to regroup, predation ceases. In a healthy population, roughly speaking, about one-third of the live-born calves reach the age of 10 months. Therefore, in the spring, a ratio of 3 to 1 cows-to-calves is appropriate to maintain herd numbers.

Elk droppings, like those of other members of the deer family, are in pellet form during the winter and fall. When spring approaches and the forage materials become more succulent and lush, the stools become somewhat flat and ill-formed, resembling a small cow pie. A hunter can thus use elk droppings to make a fairly accurate judgment as to when the elk are using a specific area.

The tracks and gait of an elk are reasonably easy to distinguish. Tracks are much larger than a deer but are small and less pointed than a moose. It can be difficult to discern elk tracks from those of cattle. Since their ranges overlap at times, study may be necessary to learn to distinguish the two. Elk tracks are a little

Most elk calves are born during the first week of June and about 30 percent will survive to reach the age of 1 year.

Through not as aquatic as moose, elk frequent a watery environment.

more pointed than those of cattle and less blocky. The lines of an elk track are finer. After following a questionable set of tracks for some distance, it should soon become apparent which species is being followed. Elk meander and traverse rough country, negotiating rocky areas and blowdown with ease. Cattle tend to avoid such country. Also, elk readily paw down through snow to reach grass while cattle will not.

An elk's gait sets it apart from other members of the deer family. When trotting, the elk holds its head horizontally and, oftentimes, above the horizontal plane of its back. Its nose is tipped slightly skyward.

Seeing a large bull trotting through an area of heavy, close timber with its nose thrust up, rolling his head from side to side, negotiating his rack through the trees, is impressive. Loud cracks are audible as dead, low-hanging branches snap.

Elk are good jumpers, making pasture fences or tangles of blowdown no obstacle. They frequently will plow through and break down fences while moving from one range to another. In addition, they are excellent swimmers and enjoy boggy, wet terrain laced with streams. They cross streams and large rivers at will; even the calves readily swim after their mothers. While photographing elk in Yellowstone Park, I have often observed numbers of them standing in streams and pawing at the water, seeming to relish the entire experience.

Elk behavior sometimes has no rhyme or reason. A good hun-

Elk droppings vary in shape and consistency depending on the time of year. Generally, they are elliptical in shape and larger than those of a deer.

ting pal, John Wozniak, had spotted a band of cows, calves and one spike bull as they moved across an open hillside. He followed their tracks for about 5 miles as they meandered through thick lodgepole and deep snow. The herd was unaware of John's pursuit. As their trail crossed a rocky, narrow ridge one of the elk broke off and ambled along the spine of the ridge. The ridgetop was narrow and thickly strewn with room-sized boulders. Navigating it was a formidable task and as John followed the elk to the point of the ridge, he had to pick his way with difficulty through the boulder field. The elk, however, moved through it with ease and at one spot mounted a huge, flat rock and stood for a considerable time gazing at the surrounding country. The elk's tracks indicated that it had changed positions several times as it surveyed the surrounding basins and mountains.

A herd of elk, when at ease and undisturbed, emit a variety of vocal noises and calls. Calves, even newborn ones, separated from their mothers give a high-pitched squeal which carries a considerable distance. EE-E-E UH! As a normal means of maintaining contented contact with its mother and the herd, the calf emits a similar call but softer and of shorter duration.

Cows give a call similar to the calves, but stronger, deeper, and more forceful. She will use this call to attract a wandering calf to her. A travelling band of cows and calves maintains a continuous chorus of squeals and grunts. accompanied by the noisy popping

Rubs like this are often found in country where bull elk have spent the summer or early fall months. They often completely destroy   a small tree in the process.

and snapping of brush and twigs.

All mature cow elk use a clearly audible, hoarse bark when disturbed or in a state of uncertainty. This call indicates concern but not necessarily outright fear. If the source of the concern is identified and flight is indicated, the barking is broken off. It also serves to alert the entire herd and bring it to a state of attentiveness.

Elk live to a ripe old age, especially in captivity. One zoo-raised specimen lived 19 years and 2 weeks. A wild elk in Arizona reportedly lived to the age of at least 25 years. The animal was a large bull which had been transported to Arizona from Wyoming in 1913. He was identified by the ear tag he still wore. Wild elk in the Northern Rockies probably have a much shorter life span. One cow that was trapped and ear-tagged near the Spotted Bear Ranger Station at the north end of the Bob Marshall Wilderness in Montana was harvested in good condition at age 16 by a hunter 80 miles south of the station.

Hunters, lack of habitat, and adverse climatic conditions are some of the factors limiting life expectancy. A life span of 6 to 10 years for a wild elk is reasonably accurate.

REFERENCES CITED

5. Murie, Olaus J. *The Elk of North America*. Teton Book Shop, Jackson, Wyoming. 1979. Pp 69, 129.
6. *Records of North American Big Game*. 8th Ed. 1981, Boone and Crockett Club, Alexandria, Virginia. Pp. 162.
7. Thomas, Jack W., and Toweill, Dale E. *Elk of North America Ecology and Management*. 1982. Stackpole Books, Harrisburg, Pennsylvania. Pp. 698.

Habits and Habitat

Although elk today dwell mostly in the mountains, in early times their habitat was primarily the plains and foothills. Some populations, however, proved exceptions to the rule and spent their entire life cycle in the mountains. For instance, early trappers in the mountainous country surrounding the North Fork of the Salmon River in Idaho reported seeing large groups of elk. Favored niches in the mountains held more or less resident populations of elk that would undoubtedly migrate to lower elevations, perhaps even to the plains, during the winter months.

Mountain-dwelling elk were the exception as the Lewis and Clark Expedition learned. The group nearly starved in September 1805 while crossing the Bitterroot Range through Lolo Pass, which lies on the divide between Montana and Idaho. Even though it was early fall, there was no game to be had and the snow was very deep.

It is safe to say that massive numbers of elk formerly lived on the plains and that the entire population was driven into the mountains by advancing "civilization" in comparatively recent years.

Habitat requirements of elk are indeed complex, influenced by many factors. In the simplest of terms, there are 3 factors which elk must have to survive. The first, of course, is water. Second is a continuous source of quality forage in quantities sufficient to maintain body tissues and reproductive potential. Third, elk must have large areas of adequate escape cover. These refuge areas enable elk to interact as a species, to reproduce, to escape from the ultimate predator, man.

In certain areas elk can be found relatively close to human habitation, easily accessible to people on foot or traveling by vehicle. Human and elk ranges often overlap, especially when deep snow pushes the elk down from the high country. But unlike whitetail deer, elk must have large, isolated areas to retreat into since their tolerance for man's intrusion is limited. They must have high, isolated mountain basins, large roadless national forests, or other such sections of country off limits to humans, be they hunters or other categories of recreationists. Off limits means areas with restricted access to man or country so rugged and large that it is rarely visited by people. Such places are mandatory during the calving season.

I spent nearly 2 seasons and almost killed a horse attempting to cut a trail into an isolated basin in the Selway Bitterroot Wilderness in Montana. Previous scouting trips had revealed the presence of large numbers of elk. My companion, seeing the extreme difficulty of the country and the super effort required to pack out elk quarters, gave up the project. His parting comment was, "There should be a few places somewhere where elk are completely safe from human pressure. This is one of those places." Being naturally hardheaded and desirous of a big bull, I pressed on. But after two seasons of sawing and hacking, I failed to punch in even a crude trail suitable for horse travel.

Since I prefer to hunt alone or with one other close friend who is equally crazy about elk hunting, I settled on a backpacking bowhunt into the basin. It was, I'll admit, a fantastic hunt. We saw 7 very good bulls and numerous cows in the 5 days. We had the opportunity to observe a rutting bull and 12 cows in the alpine scrub near the head of the basin for more than an hour early one morning. He would lay his dark, ivory-tipped rack back over his shoulders and bugle every few minutes while working his cows. We were completely captivated by the band's interaction.

A day later at dusk, we spotted a huge bull half a mile away across the basin. When we first spotted him, with our naked eye, he was standing in an avalanche chute, raking small lodgepole pine with his rack. After expressing several grunts and gasps while glassing the bull, I decided he was the biggest-bodied bull elk I had ever personally seen, Yellowstone elk included. An accurate determination of the size of his antlers was not practical as the distance was too great and the light fading. Suffice it to say, I could see flashes of his white-tipped antler tines every time he flexed his mighty neck as he destroyed the surrounding real

During the winter months, elk attempt to conserve energy at every opportunity, even traveling single file during migrations through deep snow.

estate.

Over the course of the hunt, I came to realize the futility of taking a bull in this country. It would indeed take a Herculean effort to backpack a trophy and meat out of this high country. Warm weather and meat spoilage during archery season are problems to be dealt with, too. I'm still trying to find a solution to these difficulties. Maybe my companion was right. Perhaps there should be places big bulls can find ultimate seclusion.

All wild creatures must learn to adapt to their environment. They must live by the constraints presented by their surroundings and take advantage of opportunities. Elk do this quite well even though they have been forced to live in a small fraction of their original range. These learned lessons are conditioned into their genetic structure and passed off to their offspring, continually improving the species. The weak, infirm, and nonadaptable are lost. Natural selection insures that their deficiences are not passed on.

Elk show their adaptability when they bring absolutely all unnecessary activity to a halt during the tough winter months of December, January and February in an effort to conserve energy. I once photographed a lone bull in late January that had holed up for the winter along the course of a small stream. The snow was very deep, about 3 and a half feet, and the only available forage was along the stream bank where the flowing water had cut under the snow, uncovering a small strip of grass. The bull would stand in the stream and feed by cocking his head to the side, his antlers, in some places, raking the snow on the opposite bank. I watched the bull for several days, being careful not to disturb him, and observed that he would move no more than 50 yards per day. His only energy output involved moving from his bed to the creek. He often sought the rays of sunshine that filtered through the trees. Thus, he took advantage to conserve energy while maintaining life. Elk being mixed feeders, he would even feed on unpalatable spruce needles from time to time. I wished him luck in his struggle.

Contemporary elk are very alert and extremely difficult to approach in the wild since they are conditioned to man's intrusions. They are essentially herd animals, which further complicates their ability to be approached. Posture and body language of alarmed herd members serve to alert other members of the band to danger. Herding is an excellent anti-predator strategy.

An elk's eyesight is comparable to other members of the deer family, adequate but not their best-developed sense. Their nose and ears work superbly. I personally believe an elk's sense of smell foils more hunts than any other sense they possess. At the close ranges demanded by bowhunters, scent is especially critical. Many times bulls are bugled to within close range and then, suddenly without warning or sound, they melt off into the timber.

My hunting partner, John Wozniak, while hunting elk near Wisdom, Montana, glassed a herd of elk about 1,000 yards distant. The elk were taking their leisure in a small, wet, lightly-wooded draw. The herd members were in various degrees of repose. Some were grazing contentedly while others were bedded, chewing their cuds. It was during archery season and John had slipped to within 30 yards of the resting herd. A bull could be heard bugling sporadically in the distance, but this had no effect on the cows. As John studied the scene a large cow began feeding toward his position and would shortly present a close shot.

Now John keeps a small feather tied to the end of his bow to continually monitor the wind direction. As luck would have it, the wind abruptly shifted toward the oncoming cow and she and the relaxed herd (John emphasizes instantly) were on their feet and gone.

When the calves are born in the spring, the elk are scattered or in small groups of two or three. As soon as the calves can travel the bands reform, so in the summer the groups consist of cows, calves and young bulls. The mature bulls are alone or in small

Mature elk can paw through considerable accumulation of snow to reach grass.

groups at this time. During the September rut, the herds consist of bulls, cows and calves. The bands are relatively small because the herd bull can manage only a limited number of cows. Outcast young bulls and spikes will frequent the fringes of the herd bull's harem of cows. During the winter, the bulls tend to wander off alone or in small groups while the bands of cows and calves are small so as to not overload the food supply in any one place.

Next to reproductive urges and nutritional requirements, the weather and climatic conditions probably have the greatest continual influence on elk behavior. Elk can survive, and indeed be unaffected, by extremely cold temperatures. However, if very cold temperatures are accompanied by deep snow and lack of forage, problems arise. Elk have evolved several techniques of coping with inclement weather conditions that may go on for several weeks before breaking. The animals are stimulated by weather changes and adjust their biological rhythms accordingly, no matter what the season of the year. Temperature variations in excess of 100 degrees Fahrenheit can occur in the Northern Rockies in a matter of 24 to 48 hours.

With the onset of true winter, elk attempt, whenever possible, to conserve energy while maintaining their normal body state. Every motion is calculated, purposeful. Leg and body movements are slow and deliberate. Distances between bedding and feeding sites are minimal. If a short or long migration is

Increased access to elk habitat via logging roads poses a serious problem to elk populations.

necessary to locate new food supplies, the elk travel in single file with each succeeding animal enjoying progressively easier travel.

Wind has a major effect on the activity and movements of elk. Wind greatly accelerates their radiated heat loss by removing the tiny layer of heated air surrounding the body. The animals, therefore, seek out dense stands of evergreens which afford some protection. Additionally, a dense stand of conifers acts somewhat as a thermal cover, creating a "mini-climate" favorable to the elk. Such areas provide protection from the elements with the least expenditure of energy. Wind also hampers the ability of elk to interpret sounds in their surroundings, making them reluctant to move about. Researcher Robert Beall found that elk are prone to seek shelter when wind speeds were greater than 30 miles per hour.

Elk will, if necessary, wander long distances, meandering through the trees to locate proper bedding sites. Using favorable topographical features of the land and utilization of the sun's rays are the only means elk have, other than body adaptations, (e.g., hair growth, etc.) to cope with the temperature and weather fluctuations in their environment.

Mature bulls must feed more heavily than cows during the summer months so as to build fat reserves for the coming rut. Doing so maximizes the time devoted to mating during the rut. However, as feeding time is minimized and energy expenditures increase, the bull may lose a lot of his fat reserves during the rut. The supply of fat reserves left after the rut determines the likelihood of the bull surviving the winter. The bull must be genetically conditioned to seek out and consume the best quality forages during the spring and summer months.

Herd dispersal is another method elk use to decrease pressure on available food supplies and make use of a wider area of their range. Locating suitable pockets of adequate forage and favorable "mini-climates" will insure the survival of some individuals and bands of elk. Elk that are not able to find such favorable survival areas may perish.

Elk also face competition for food, especially when on winter range. Bands of elk, during the winter months, are forced by deepening snows to drop into country inhabited by cattle and man. Domestic stock and elk can exert considerable pressure on grass forage supplies. In western Montana, there is a serious problem with elk eating winter supplies of hay reserved for cattle. When problems occur, hunts are held to harvest the offending elk and scatter the herds, thus minimizing the damage. In difficult winters with prolonged periods of extreme cold coupled with deep snows (such as occurred in the Northern Rockies in 1983), the antelope, deer, and elk all compete for hard-to-obtain forage.

Man, too, must be dealt with by the elk. Winter ranges often are in close proximity to urban developments. As a result, snowmobilers, crosscountry skiers and other outdoor enthusiasts can disturb elk, causing them to abandon their winter range or at least disturb their feeding routine. In trying to escape man's harassment, elk use precious energy reserves causing them to weaken and thereby decreasing their chance of winter survival.

The heat of summer causes other problems for these large animals. Since elk are relatively intolerant of heat, they seek dense, damp stands of timber on north-facing slopes where the air temperature begins to rise. Bogs, cedar swamps, and generally shady, cool areas are favorite summer habitats. With food easy to obtain and in good supply during the hot months, it becomes unnecessary for elk to range far. Little movement keeps production of body heat to a minimum.

Migration is an integral part of the life cycle of elk that live in the mountainous regions. Often the movement involves more change in elevation than long lateral distance. This, in part, is because man's infringement on open land at lower elevations forces the animals to seek, when possible, relatively undisturbed habitat found only in the higher mountains.

Snow is the chief motivator of elk migration. Generally speaking, snow cover deep enough to impede feeding is necessary to trigger large-scale migration. Downward migration stops or slows

Dense stands of "dog-hair" lodgepole pine provide adequate escape cover for elk. Bulls have an uncanny ability to maneuver their huge racks through the thickets.

when snow-free forage is found. Because the movements take place in response to the weather, exact times of migration are unpredictable.

Occasionally, migration routes cover considerable distance and follow a predetermined pattern year after year. Elk calves following their mothers become familiar with travel patterns and continue them. In western Montana and northern Idaho, migration routes are reasonably short. However, elk are capable of changing these traditional migration routes in response to hunting pressure or advancing human habitation. This is a tribute to their adaptability.

One factor which has had a profound effect on elk movements and migration of elk throughout the Northern Rockies is logging.

Use of logging roads by hunters, four-wheel drive enthusiasts, firewood gatherers and recreationists pushes the animals into still more remote areas to seek refuge from man. Once an area is logged, it may never again provide the security and avenues of travel available to elk before cutting.

In the spring, migration patterns are reversed and commence with the new growth of vegetation. Elk follow the browse line back to isolated calving areas. Here they remain until the coming of deep snow again forces them down.

Mature elk can move easily in powder snow to depths of three feet. Deeper snow greatly reduces their ability to move about and to paw away snow cover to reach food. Calves from the previous spring have difficulty maneuvering in snow depths of two and one-half feet. Aerial studies indicate elk prefer a snow depth of less than two feet.

As I write this in December 1983, western Montana is in the grip of severe arctic-like conditions. Extreme night-time temperatures of minus 20 to 30 degrees Fahrenheit have persisted for more than 2 weeks. At 4,900 feet elevation, the snow depth is 34 inches on the level. The elk and deer are already hard pressed and have migrated from the wilderness area behind my home. They have dropped 1,000 to 1,500 feet in elevation and traveled roughly 6 miles. I viewed the herd just this morning feeding not 1 mile from a major east-west interstate highway and in view of several houses. I'm concerned as there are still two more months of winter ahead.

An elk's diet in winter is influenced by what's available. In areas such as northern Idaho, elk feed primarily on winter shrubs, while in western Montana the diet will consist of browse-type shrubs and grass which are exposed on south-facing slopes. Grass is preferred, if available. But as the snow cover deepens, elk turn to taller browse-type plants. In very deep snow elk may be forced to go to conifer browse. With the receding snow line of spring and summer, elk turn to new grass growth. Grass constitutes a major source of forage for elk during these months, while forbs such as elk thistle, fireweed, and common cow parsnip also can be a large part of the diet.

The herd normally will begin feeding each day shortly before daylight and continue for 2 to 3 hours. The animals then retire to a bedding site, usually a dense stand of conifers offering favorable wind currents and some view. The bedding and feeding areas are chosen by a trail-wise cow. The midday period is spent at ease ruminating and resting. Shortly before dark, the elk again graze, usually in the same area unless a disturbance has occurred. Feeding and resting constitute more than 90 percent of an elk's daily routine except during the rut, periods of inclement weather, or when human activity disrupts daily patterns.

The ability and instinct of elk to adjust feeding routines is well developed. For instance, in periods of very cold weather, elk greatly increase feeding times for two reasons. First, maintaining body heat causes food to be metabolized more quickly and requires more calories. Second, the physical act of moving about in search of the food stimulates heat production and helps the animal maintain a normal body core temperature.

When being pursued, elk secrete themselves in dense stands of timber which provides a barrier between themselves and the predator, satisfying their security needs. How far elk run after being disturbed by humans varies a great deal according to location, conditioning of the elk, and type of escape cover available. How close an elk can be approached by man also depends on these factors. If shooting has occurred in the proximity of an elk, it may run as far as 3 to 8 miles, particularly if the animal has been repeatedly disturbed. Solitary elk, especially trophy bulls, tend to flee longer distances than do groups.

I once worked my way into an isolated pocket of timber along a stream in a small, secluded basin that rarely got hunted. As I left the trail to set up a camp by the creek, a bull stood up and nonchalantly walked off into the timber, crossing a small opening as he ambled away. He probably had been in the basin all summer, undisturbed by man, thus giving him little fear of humans.

An elk will not go as far if escape cover is very dense with heavy amounts of blowdown that create a barrier between the elk and the intruder. Other factors that shorten flight distance are deep snow, exhaustive effort, and ability to put large physical barriers such as ravines and ridges between themselves and a disturbance.

Elk as a species have the uncanny ability to use cover very effectively to conceal themselves at the slightest sense of danger. The stories are legend of bulls coming nicely to the bugling hunter — closer and closer. A brow tine here, a piece of rump patch there. Just a few more steps...and poof, gone, as silently and quickly as a puff of smoke on a windy day. Such is elk hunting.

REFERENCES CITED

8. Beall, R.C. 1974. *Winter Habitat Selection and Use by a Western Montana Elk Herd*. Ph.d. Thesis, University of Montana. Pp. 197.

The Rut

Heavy frost blanketed the tent and covered the equipment lying in disorganized order about the camp. A small, cheery fire warmed numbed fingertips. As preparations were quietly being made, anxious eyes would gaze up the timbered ridge that was outlined by a thousand glimmering stars. Each ear was tuned toward the fringes of the small ring of firelight — listening. Suddenly it came, causing all human movement to freeze so as not in interrupt the sound. It was beautiful, clear, and high pitched as it gained in volume and gusto. Ooh-h-h-h-e-e-e-E-E-E-E-a-h-h! The bugle originated deep in the bull elk's massive chest, started low and increased in intensity, higher and higher into a shriek, then trailed off into silence. A delightful chill flashed up the spines of the two veteran hunters as they smiled at each other. It was September 15th, the opening morning of elk season. A long time had passed since the last hunt.

Far and away the most exciting time to hunt elk is during the rut in the fall. It's not necessarily the most productive time, but it is exciting. This reproductive period for the animals causes increased activity and a higher degree of visibility. From their isolated summer and fall pasturages, the bulls, now fat and prime, seek out cows and gather them into groups. Oftentimes a dominant bull gathers cows simply by taking charge of a group of cows, driving younger bulls from the herd. The males become less attentive to their surroundings and go for long periods of time feeding on very little.

The exact meaning and function of the elk bugle is not fully understood but is a large part of the mystique and aesthetics of elk hunting.

It is a fantastic time of the year in the Northern Rockies. Cold, frosty nights are stealing life from the foliage of the aspen, western larch, and huckleberry bushes. Slopes are clothed in hues of red and gold. The air is clear, clean and invigorating. It chills the nose and lips as you breathe in, while the exhaled air shoots out plumes of fog. Skim ice along the edges of streams clearly indicates a seasonal change; for the elk it is a season of great importance.

Sportsmen disagree about what actually stimulates bulls to begin the rutting period. I've frequently heard: "The bull's aren't bugling because there hasn't been a hard frost or the weather has been too warm." This theory is erroneous. Research has clearly shown that certain neuroendocrine mechanisms stimulate a bull to breed and a cow to come into estrus.

The sequence of events is linked to the length of day and the amount of sunlight striking the retina of the eye. In reaction to light stimulus, a specific gland, the pineal, releases a hormone that activates the pituitary gland. The pituitary, in turn, secretes a hormone that causes the testicular tissue to produce testosterone. testosterone then stimulates semen production and rouses the breeding urge.

This activity is nature's way of ensuring a calf crop even in years of very mild autumns when severe weather may not come

With the onset of the September rut, the mature bulls are consumed with a desire to herd cows. Perpetuation of the species is his main aim.

until well into the winter. The length of day and night, luckily, never vary from year to year.

A dominant breeding bull will attempt to attract and hold a number of cows since there are fewer males than females in a given population. This instinctive behavior allows for many cows to be serviced by few bulls that need exert only a minimum amount of effort. Additionally, a cow in estrus, or heat, will attract a number of bulls from the surrounding area. This serves to increase the level of competition among males for breeding rights and assures most of the breeding will be done by genetically superior bulls. Also, the presence of a number of bulls gives the cow an opportunity to select the most competent and vigorous bull to breed her, insuring that quality genes are passed on to her calf.

Antler size and number of points affect a bull's attractiveness to cows. The cow recognizes and acknowledges a superior set of antlers, which are an indicator of the vigor and health of the bull. Their development is, in part, a result of his ability to locate and consume a higher quality forage. Likewise, antler size and mass advertises a bull's rank and dominance among his peers.

Substantial evidence shows that breeding bulls attract cows by bugling. In fact, attracting females may be a major reason for the call. In general, the larger and more dominant the bull, the deeper and more commanding is his bugle. A lone bull seeking cows will bugle with great volume and a full repertoire of sounds, competing with other bulls to attract the attention of cows in the vicinity. Cows are attracted, sight unseen, to the bull with the best voice.

The high-pitched sound of a full bugle will travel long distances through light timber and open alpine parks. It is in this type of country that much of the rutting activity takes place. With his neck extended or turned, the bull methodically raises his chin and head to a horizontal plane on a level with, or slightly below, his shoulder hump. The bull then opens his mouth and retracts his lips, almost curling the upper lip backward. The tongue is slightly retracted and the incisor teeth are visible. Exhaled air rushes up the trachea, over the vocal cords, and out the mouth with each area playing a part in forming the bugling sound. A bull is capable of making a wide variety of squeals, yelps, coughs, and grunts as well as the chilling bugle.

Some researchers believe bugling is used as a means to attract a mate, and it does occur most frequently when cows are active and feeding. Early pre-dawn hours and just before and after sunset are peak bugling times.

A rutting bull in the company of cows uses a lower pitched grunt or yelps rather than a full bugle. The sound is repeated several times in succession and may be written E-E-E-eunk-eunk-eunk. This call performs a number of functions. It serves to reassure the cows in his possession of his masculinity and power. It also develops and strengthens a social bond between the bull and his cows. Lower in volume, the shorter grunt won't carry as far as a bugle and will fail to attract an answer from wandering bulls. Such an answer might be attractive to his cows. Bull elk readily answer the bugles of other bulls in an attempt to out-advertise their competitors and put themselves in a position to attract cows. In the right circumstances, breeding bulls can be susceptible to artificial bugling which is a favored hunting technique.

Herd bulls seek to silence free-ranging bulls that are not guarding a harem. Fearful of losing cows to the bugling of another bull, the herd bull is induced to either move his harem from the area or challenge the interloper and drive him away. Following either course, the herd bull will continue bugling to reinforce his hold on his cows, especially if the outlying bull continues to bugle.

A herd bull offers the cows protection from continual harassment by younger bulls. Finding peace in his presence, they will be more contented and less likely to leave. A bull can be gentle or aggressive in his techniques of herding his cows. A wandering

An elk wallow indicates the presence of a mature bull in the area. Wallows are located in prime elk habitat.

cow's state of contentment is influenced by whether she is gently nudged back into line by the bull's body or raked by his antlers.

It is important to note that opinions vary as to the true purpose of bugling. Many game biologists and sportsmen express the view that bugling is a means of communication from one bull to the next which says: "I'm tough. Stay away from me and my cows." It's a means of stating, in as commanding a voice as possible, a bull's rank and status to others in the area. However, I've heard of instances in which cows have responded to human bugling. This would support the attraction theory. Much is yet to be learned, but personally I feel the purpose of bugling is a combination of both theories.

Bulls also have other means of advertising their presence in a given place. A wallow indicates the area is being frequented by a mature bull. The wallow is made in a swampy, wet area sometimes in the bed of a small spring or seep. Usually in August the bull selects a suitable site and begins to dig the ground with his antlers. The hole is deepened and widened by pawing at and rolling in the depression. The wallow area can be quite large, covering an area 16 feet square. The wallow pool proper can be as large as 10 square feet.

Vegetation in the immediate proximity of the wallow pool will be rubbed and torn, while the entire area may have a musky, "elkie" odor.

The types of vegetation rubbed and the amount of real estate destroyed will indicate the size and aggressiveness of the bull.

The purpose of a wallow is not fully understood. Some speculate it serves to cool the "rutting fever" or is a method of marking territory.7 Preceding and during the rut, bulls will at times lie in a wallow, mud-caked, for long periods of time. They frequently bugle without even bothering to rise. Bulls tend to return to the same wallow during successive rutting periods.

Mature rutting bulls have a very distinct, pungent, musky odor that resembles a barnyard smell. The odor announces a bull's presence for long distances with the right wind conditions. That odor has two sources. As a bull bugles, he opens his preorbital glands which are seen as deep folds or creases in the skin just in front of and below the eye. They are full of a thick, dark brown, waxy material that has a very strong odor. The more bugling a bull does, the more odor he releases. Also, after rubbing and stripping the bark off a sapling with his antlers, a bull will rub his face on the naked tree to "odorize" it. (See photo on the cover of this book.) Urine is the other source of the odor. At the termination of a bugle, the bull palpitates or throbs his penis and sheath, then sprays urine toward his belly hair. The throbbing of the genital area can easily be seen from 40 to 50 yards away. A bull may lower his head between his front legs to spray urine on his neck and mane.

Horning of vegetation is yet another way a bull makes his presence known to cows or other bulls. It is done repeatedly and

The pre-orbital gland is located in a deep skin-fold just below the eye. It contains a thick, waxy, odiferous material used to "mark" a bull's presence.

at random   during the rut. All types of vegetative growth fall victim to this display of dominance. A bull will gore grassy, damp sites, pitching clods of sod and grass high over his head. All varieties of small shrubs and bushes receive the bull's attention. A large bull won't hesitate to attack trees up to eight inches in diameter, sometimes completely girdling the tree and killing it.

Last season I found a spot in a wet stand of spruce trees that had been completely demolished by a bull which I never had the good fortune to see. The area was about 20 by 30 feet in size. In the middle stood a spruce tree, four inches in diameter, totally stripped of bark and branches from eight inches above the ground to a height of six and a half feet. The stark-white tree had several gore marks and broken limbs up to the level of eight and a half feet. The ground looked like a logging crew had begun an operation. It was trampled bare of living vegetation and had been gored repeatedly. The surrounding brush had not only been broken, but much of it had been ripped out by the roots. A number of puddles of odiferous urine were visible. I studied the spot carefully, speculating on what such a bull would look like.

Out of necessity, a bull elk is a herding animal, working to keep his group of cows from wandering. This is a full-time task for the herd bull and takes much energy. Concurrently, he must be able to identify and breed receptive cows. It is little wonder that the rutting period, which generally lasts the month of September, can be debilitating to the bull.

A straying cow will elicit a dominance display from the bull. Neck extended, ears back, and antlers laid back along his shoulders and flanks, the bull rushes the errant cow at a side angle while emitting a series of coughs and grunts. After successfully herding a cow, the bull often bugles, leaving his imprint on the cow and further conditioning her to him. I have witnessed a herd bull's utter frustration in trying to hold together a band of edgy cows. Madly running through the timber and across talus slides, he demonstrated his dominance posture in an attempt to hold his wandering cow.

As a cow reaches estrus, the bull assumes a different attitude toward her by demonstrating a breeding posture. He will approach the cow from the rear with antlers held high. He carries his ears forward. His tongue audibly flops about in his mouth between frequently lip lipping. He will attempt to lick the cow's genital area to test her receptiveness and to stimulate her to urinate. If she does, the urine is quickly licked and smelled by the bull. A special organ in the bull's mouth detects the odors of estrus, if present. After smelling the urine, the bull maintains a rather dazed look, with eyes glassed over, head thrown back, and upper lip retracted, exposing the upper palate. This posture,

Serious fighting to establish dominance is unusual among bulls. Only if both bulls are nearly equal in horn mass and body size will potentially fatal battles occur.

the purpose of which is unknown, is held for several seconds. If the cow is receptive, breeding will occur. If not, she will move off and reject the bull's advances.

The breeding technique of the bull is interesting, but rarely observed. He mounts the cow and grasps her in the loins with his front legs, which hang down along the cow's sides. Most of the bull's weight is carried on his back legs. Copulation occurs as the bull simultaneously thrusts his pelvis forward and his head and neck back. The action is quite violent, usually pushing the cow ahead and out from under the bull.

Confrontation among the males is inevitable in a species that keeps such a high profile. A bull is quickly alerted when a competitor moves into his territory. Altercations occur, but most run-ins consist of considerable posturing and bluffing. Bulls must be nearly equal in body size and antler mass for a real battle to ensue.

I have photographed elk in the rut at close range for 6 consecutive years and have yet to record a monumental battle. Severe battles do occur, occasionally, between mature breeding bulls with one or both being severely injured and killed. However, posturing and bluffing are an efficient way to husband energy. The cost in tissue reserves would be great indeed if a fight resulted at every meeting of the bulls. Animals would be hopelessly depleted and at risk to survive the rigors of the approaching winter; evolution has taught elk to avoid a fight when encounters occur among bulls.

On a recent photo trip, I worked my way into the midst of a rutting frenzy. It was a beautiful, clear morning with the air temperature at about 24 degrees Fahrenheit. Several good bulls were bugling and milling about in a small sagebrush flat that was cut by a small stream and rimmed by patches of lodgepole pine, in which a number of cows were hidden.

It was just after dawn. The bulls were literally working themselves into a real heat. I anxiously anticipated taking some excellent photographs, perhaps even catching a coveted fight scene. As I sat down to await developments, 2 heavy-beamed 6x6 bulls suddenly erupted from the trees and charged into the sagebrush. They trotted parallel to each other, a few feet apart, for more than 100 yards, both bugling every few seconds. Each was attempting to intimidate the other by displaying his body mass and antler size. Both bulls swept their antlers in short arcs just above the ground as they ran. Suddenly, at a signal known only to them, the bulls simultaneously stopped their march, faced each other and clashed. I envisioned a monumental battle of a lifetime between these animals that were nearly equal in size, but much to my disappointment the 2 bulls, after some minor pushing and shoving, continued their parallel march until they were out of sight.

Even when a battle does occur, the victorious bull seldom pursues the vanquished. Most fights are short in duration, lasting only a few minutes at the longest. Attacks are terminated by the loser simply disengaging his antlers and quickly leaving the country. The winner doesn't pressure or punish the yielding bull, but will emit a bugle in the direction of the fleeing loser.

Thoughts on Elk Hunting

The science of elk hunting is complex. Nearly every person who hunts elk on a regular basis forms opinions and beliefs of his own. Experience, being the good teacher it is, is very important to consistently score with elk. The other option, of course, is to hunt using the services of a competent guide. To be successful hunting elk on one's own, much thought and preparation must precede the hunt. There are the lucky few hunters who wander at random in the woods or road hunt and kill bull elk. They rarely take elk on a regular basis, or even rarer still, take a trophy.

My personal philosophy about elk hunting begins from the premise that a wild elk is a magnificent beast. It is with the greatest pleasure and enjoyment that I hunt them. But I enjoy elk 12 months a year, not only while hunting. It also is enjoyable to simply photograph or observe them. Elk live in wild, rugged country, inhabiting the most remote, isolated land left in the Lower 48. To pursue a premiere game animal in such habitat is a privilege and an honor. I have harvested all types and sizes of elk — calves, cows, spikes and older bulls. As I mature in years and hunting seasons, I find I derive increased pleasure in seeking a good representative bull in the most remote country I can locate. In my opinion, to take a bull elk, or any elk for that matter, from the road or by any means other than a one-on-one test of skills and instincts is a sacrilege.

Research, personal experience and discussions with ex-

Hunting elk in their natural habitat is emotionally stimulating as well as challenging.

perienced, successful elk hunters convinced me that four common denominators must be followed to consistently succeed at seeing or collecting trophy bulls. They are, in order of importance: wind strength and direction, penetrating into isolated, difficult terrain, preseason scouting, and a thorough knowledge of elk and their habits.

WIND

Wind currents in a mountain environment tend to rise in the morning as the sun warms the basins and to fall in the evening as the air cools. In the evening, as the sun sinks behind the ridgetops, the air cools very quickly and can cause abrupt changes in wind direction. These are general guidelines, but winds in timbered pockets and on open ridges can change direction suddenly and often, any time during the day. This must be constantly kept in mind. Some means of monitoring ongoing wind current conditions is critical to succeed, particularly when working in close to elk.

One method of keeping track of wind changes is to tie a small downy feather to a jacket sleeve or a bow limb. The feather will detect the slightest wind change and allow adjustments to be made while stalking. A second idea is to carry a cigarette lighter and use it frequently. The flame will bend in the slightest breeze.

The elk's most dependable line of defense is its sense of smell. With it, they sort out potential dangers. It rarely fails them. This fact must be acknowledged and dealt with effectively to successfully hunt elk. One whiff of man's scent creates instant concern, for there is no other smell like it in the elk's natural world. It commands the elk to do one thing — escape.

An elk's eyes and ears are important for picking up warning signals, but these senses are not nearly as reliable as its nose.

During its normal daily activities, an elk will hear strange cracks, thumps, and various noises which occur naturally in a living forest. An elk may not bolt at the first out-of-place sound it hears — electing rather to sort out the noise and attempt to identify it.

An elk's eyes quickly detect sudden motions. But again, such motions are part of the natural setting. A clump of snow falling with a thump off an evergreen bough or a tree limb blown by a gust of wind are causes of alarm, but usually do not induce panicked flight.

Elk may react to man's scent with controlled flight or uncontrolled panic, depending on the strength of the smell. The closer the source of the scent, the less the dilution factor and thus the stronger the elk's reaction. On the other hand, a few

An elk's sense of hearing and sight are well developed, but its sense of smell is its primary line of defense.

Elk inhabit the most pristine, rugged country left in the Lower 48.

molecules of human scent inhaled into an elk's nose tells it that danger is around, but not too close. A controlled exit is in order.

I once got caught by an errant gust of wind as a cow elk approached me down a well-used trail. I felt the 3-second puff of wind at the back of my neck and I watched for her reaction. Very soon she stopped with ears pricked forward. Her nose tilted to her left. I could follow the direction of the wind as the elk, in one smooth motion, caught the scent with her nose and followed it with a sweeping arc of her head, over her left shoulder. In just a fleeting second, she interpreted, cataloged and reacted to the scent stimulus. She evaporated into the timber. A lesson learned!

ISOLATED DIFFICULT TERRAIN

Pursuing elk in their nature environment is pure pleasure. Their home range is aesthetically pleasing to the eye and invigorating to travel through. Hunting in these mountain strongholds is a rewarding experience — with a price. The dues are sweat, broken equipment, aching muscles and, with some hunts, total exhaustion. Elk are big, rugged animals that live in big, rugged country. Mental toughness and physical preparedness are required to be one of the 14 of 100 hunters who take elk each season. High altitudes, acres of crotch-busting blowdown, and hundreds of yards of ankle-twisting rock slides

The heavy beamed trophies are still around but are difficult to collect.

September is a great time to be in the Northern Rockies. The sky is azure blue and the air crisp and clean.

must be crossed in order to penetrate into the "right" kind of elk habitat. "Right" means country so isolated and demanding that few other people hunt there. It may be a large tract of tough country or it may be a relatively small piece of rugged country surrounded by less demanding habitat. Country that tests one's resolve and determination is the "right" habitat.

To be successful, an elk hunter must maintain a reasonable conditioning program that is a way of everyday life. Without such fitness, it's impossible to penetrate into prime elk country. Attempting to condition oneself in the month or week prior to a hunt is folly. Even worse is no conditioning at all.

Mental toughness is equally as important as physical conditioning. If the mind is beaten, all is lost; if the body is beaten, the mind can make it go on. How badly do you want an elk or trophy bull? What price will you pay? The price will usually be high if a trophy is to be taken.

For example, let me relate the following story. I had invited 2 friends, Bob Bently and Paul Myers, to join me for a backpack elk hunting trip. The bowhunt took place during the September bugling season. Two months before the hunt, I strongly advised them to get into top shape because the trip would be over 9 tough miles, 4 of which would be crosscountry with no trail. I impressed upon them the success of their hunt would hinge on the condition of their legs, lungs and backs.

Bob made an attempt to comply and arrived from Florida in relatively good condition, albeit a little overweight. Paul is slender but had done little or nothing to prepare for the hunt. He was also a smoker. The trip in was probably the most gruelling project Paul had ever undertaken.

We all carried 70-pound-plus packs. The terrain soon began to take its toll on them. At rest stops, Paul was so exhausted that he immediately would shed his pack and curl into the fetal position to fall asleep instantly. After 6 miles, we were coaxing Paul to just put one foot ahead of the other and to look ahead toward one goal at a time. Bob and I were becoming concerned about Paul's condition. His cheeks were flushed and his breath came in rapid, shallow gasps. We slowed our pace considerably to accommodate Paul and eventually reached a suitable campsite 3 miles short of our goal. Paul, after feeding on a steak and sweets, quickly fell asleep.

The next day we did reach our primary camp, but the entire hunt was conducted in a lower key than I'd hoped for. We saw plenty of shootable bulls, but were unable to push hard enough to make a connection. Paul earned a great deal of respect from all of us on that hunt. Using every drop of mental discipline and intestinal fortitude he possessed, he didn't quit. Paul dug very deep for the strength that enabled him to make the trip into camp.

Getting into a secluded patch of timber isn't necessarily the most difficult part of a hunt. Once an elk is down, the real work begins. The piper must be paid. It is no, and I emphasize no, easy feat to pack elk quarters or boned meat out of the mountains. Antlers, capes, and meat weighing a total of 350 to 450 pounds, must be transported over undulating, steep, rocky country. Horses, of course, help solve the problem but it isn't uncommon to be unable to reach the carcass with a horse. Backpacking hunts present a problem because all the meat must be moved by leg, lung and back power.

Various publications have lauded the benefits of backpacking elk hunts, but this type of hunt is not for everyone. Glorious pictures show the successful hunter highlighted by the setting sun with a beautiful cape and antlers neatly strapped to his pack frame. With gun in hand, hat sitting neatly on a sweat-free brow, this presents an idyllic picture. Reality is much, much different. Packing out elk parts is dirty, tough, time-consuming work that ceases to be fun in a hurry. Obviously, the situation calls for determination, dedication and mental toughness. Personal satisfaction after the task is completed is a satisfying moment in-

A bull in heavy timber, where they often retreat to hide when pressured by hunters.

deed.

A close hunting friend told me about an interesting packing innovation this past season. Frank had downed a high-scoring bull in deep snow 5 miles from the road. He butchered the bull and proceeded to pack out one unboned quarter per trip. By the time he started the long ascent up the final slope to the truck, Frank had worked up quite a sweat even though the temperature was around 10 degrees. As he painstakingly worked the 100-pound quarters up the mountain, he beat the heat by taking off one layer of clothing, piece by piece, every quarter mile or so. He hung them on bushes along his route. When he reached the road, he was down to his long underwear. Then, as he returned for the next quarter and had begun to chill, he simply collected his clothes and layered them back on as he found them. He repeated the procedure 4 times.

PRE-SEASON SCOUTING

I have lived and hunted in western Montana for seven years and have just, in the last 2 or 3 years, begun to feel I have a handle on the country. I can now hunt certain spots and consistently get into elk. This follows many conversations with knowledgeable people, a great deal of walking and grunting up and down mountains, and map study.

Studying topographical and general Forest Service maps is helpful in locating good hunting grounds. Map evaluation will show road locations, land elevations, trails, and where wet, boggy spots are situated.

If one is so inclined, a reputable guide can provide the same services. In my opinion, do-it-yourself hunts are exciting, challenging, and can be very rewarding. However, much homework must be done if the do-it-your-selfer is to bag an animal.

It is wise to gain as thorough a knowledge as possible of the country to be hunted. Map study and conversations with locals will do for a start, but there is no substitute for good old leg work. As many pre-hunt days as possible should be spent in the area to be hunted, observing game movements, studying wind current tendencies, and understanding the lay of game trails. The hunter will soon develop an overall picture of the elks' location and habits, allowing a hunt to be planned with direction and some degree of confidence. This confidence will spawn a positive mental attitude that says, "Taking an elk is within the realm of possibility and may be a probability." A positive mental attitude is a good deal of the battle. It can make a backpack seem a lot lighter and the trail not so steep.

While scouting, be discreet and low key. It is important to keep fires small, work the fringes of prime habitat, keep a distance from sighted elk, and make the entire trip of short duration.

Besides physically exploring their habitat, using binoculars is one of the most important parts of meaningful scouting. Early morning and late evening sessions with high quality binoculars offer the best chance to see and chart elk movements. Long periods spent at various vantage points will unlock a wealth of information concerning the activities of the animals.

Elk usually don't move much from their summer and fall haunts until pushed by hunters or weather. Like other members of the deer family they live a life of predictable routine. They visit the same feeding grounds, water in the same creeks, and travel the same trails unless forced to change.

The lay of the land should be studied intently. First impressions are often not the best nor do they show the entire picture. Two or three consecutive days spent observing elk movements will reveal their activity. This is the backbone of a well-planned hunt. Pre-planning a hunt properly gives the hunter his best shot at filling his tag.

I realize the previous discussions are ideal ways to prepare for an elk hunt. I appreciate that there are other demands and priorities that pick at one's time. I'm a businessman and a father

This is the sort of high, beautiful Northern Rockies country in which elk are found — and which is a pleasure for the hunter to visit.

and am not naive about the number of hours in a day. I'm suggesting ways and ideas to hunt elk that may produce a favorable result. Working the suggestions into the schedule of life is probably more difficult than packing out elk quarters. Some pockets of elk habitat have taken me 2 or 3 seasons to fully understand. The time pinch wouldn't permit answering all the questions during one season. I'm very envious of my game biologist friends who derive their livelihood by spending hours upon hours walking in or flying over elk habitat during a regular "working" day. When the season starts their homework is already done, very thoroughly.

KNOWLEDGE OF ELK

An understanding of elk and their species characteristics is linked closely to the concept of pre-season scouting. Knowing habits and preferences gives a hunter an idea of what time of year to scout a certain type of country. Having enough information to anticipate an elk's next move and to out-think him, is critical. Granted, luck is an important factor when hunting any animal, but the scales of luck can be tipped your way by careful forethought.

A case in point: We were hunting near the head of a basin in which we had spotted a herd bull and several cows late one evening. The next morning, expecting the herd to be in the immediate area, we arrived just at first light. We were disappointed when we could not promptly locate the group of 12 cows and the bull. After glassing the surrounding area carefully, at about 8:30 a.m., I found the herd about three-quarters of a mile away in the head of the basin, at near 8,000 feet elevation. The cows were casually feeding as the bull drifted among them bugling frequently. The open and rocky terrain was studded with small tree-line pines. I was again amazed at the elk's ability to easily navigate difficult, steep mountain slopes. I could see the bull assume bugling posture but the distance was so great that the sound was lost. As the sun rose higher in the sky I knew the herd would bed soon and a stalk might be possible.

Soon a cow located a small, sparsely timbered, rocky draw and the herd settled down. Suddenly the basin appeared absent of game. If we had arrived late and had just begun to study the country, we would have missed the herd, but by anticipating their likely behavior at a certain time of day, in a certain location, we were able to follow them to their bedding area and plan a stalk.

One way to approach elk hunting is to think of it on a month-

An elk has a head-high gait, which distinguishes it from other members of the deer family.

by-month basis. Hunting elk in September is very different from late-November hunting. The rut and changing weather conditions as winter approaches are the two factors most affecting hunting strategies. State regulations also change from month to month. Idaho, for instance, has a general gun season while the elk are rutting. Montana, however, has restricted rifle hunts during the rut and only in certain specific hunting zones. Montana does have a general archery season during the rut. The earliest rifle hunt in Wyoming is mid-September. Regulations alone may be a deciding factor when a hunt is planned.

During mid and late September the bulls are active and do much roaming. They tend to be slightly less elusive, less observant, and more visible for longer periods during the day. Hunting during the rut can increase the odds of collecting a herd type bull.

September is a super time to hunt elk. The weather is moderate to cool, and the rut is in full swing. There is something about an elk bugle on a clear, frosty morning that is totally unforgettable and addicting. It beckons, as if to say, "I'm here, close by. Try to hunt me." A bugle signifies success. It states that a bull is near. This is the right place and time to have a chance at taking a wild elk. The bugle brings life and meaning to the hunt.

The proficient use of the artificial elk bugle to lure in a rutting bull is a very exacting art that requires much practice. Many hunters have developed the use of the bugle to a high degree.

September hunts often find the woods dry and the weather warm, creating special problems with stalking and meat spoilage.

After hearing an artificial bugle, the bull will react in one of three ways. He and his cows may move out of the vicinity. He might not move at all. Or he could move closer to the sound. Bugling with the currect frequency, pitch, and tone are important and can be learned by studying instructional tapes or working with an experienced bugler. Only practice at blowing the bugle will hone one's skill.

To describe with words the currect bugling technique would be very difficult. Each hunting situation calls for a different approach but if called correctly a bull can often be talked into very close range. Suffice it to say, bugling elk is an efficient, exciting way to hunt mature trophy bull elk. Weather conditions in September can cause mid-day lulls in the hunting activity. Afternoons become warm, with temperatures in the 50s and 60s, forcing the animals to seek shade. Since August and September are dry months that make the woods noisy, still hunting is usually a tough proposition. Tracking the elk also is unreliable this time of year because snow, even at higher elevations, is hard to find. And if snow is hard to find, so are the elk. Their colors blend in well with the autumn foliage, sighting them, particularly through binoculars at long distances, is an accomplishment in itself.

In the northern Rocky Mountain states, the general elk season is in full swing by mid to late October, which is a transition month. Early October finds the fever of the rut waning and the harems of cows beginning to scatter. The herd bulls, their breeding done, become more elusive and begin to feed heavily in preparation for winter. The weather shows definite signs of change. Daytime temperatures fall from the 40s and 50s in early October to the 30s and 40s in late October. Ice begins to close over the creeks at night. Days shorten noticeably. Snow can come to the high country during October and sometimes is heavy, making the spotting of elk with binoculars or by tracking much easier.

Severe weather conditions usually can be expected anytime in November, particularly late in the month. With November comes an entirely different set of hunting challenges. Elk are skittish since more hunters are in the woods. Inclement weather conditions begin to affect their urge to migrate, the timing of which depends on the amount of snow in the high country. If the snow is deep enough the elk begin to move to lower elevations. When they make their move, locating a major travel route and attempting an ambush is a good bet for the hunter.

Other strategies that work well are to spot animals feeding just after dawn or to find tracks in the snow and take up the chase. Spotting a group of feeding elk offers a good opportunity, if wind and cover are right, to surprise the animals since precise location

Elk, particularly mature bulls, often bed overlooking their back trail which makes surprising them difficult.

of the herd is known.

Tracking a single elk offers the supreme challenge. Analyzing track shape and size will help identify a good bull. His chosen route through or around groups of trees will indicate his rack size. Stamina and determination are necessary to track down a bull who can wander long distances with his mile-eating pace. Looking ahead frequently while tracking and moving slowly — very, very slowly — are mandatory to surprise a bull.

Bull elk bed often, choosing sites that look over their back trail. While in these beds elk are difficult to see, giving them a definite advantage over the hunter.

Because of deep snow and intense cold, serious late-season elk hunting can be painful and cause much suffering. Sudden, severe blizzards and short days can complicate the hunt. While tracking it's a good idea to take notice of the time. Heavy cloud cover that blots out the sun makes it easy to get confused about time. I once returned to camp thinking it was near dark, but it turned out to be only 3 o'clock in the afternoon. More dangerous would be to get caught away from camp at nightfall.

One must always be prepared for the worst. An elk hunter who goes afield with any regularity will eventually get caught out in severe, unexpected weather and be forced to stay the night. It's not a question of if one will get caught out. It's a question of when and how bad will it be. The outcome will depend on planning and preparation. It is sound policy to never, never, go elk hunting without having emergency supplies in a daypack. Even during September hunts, when the days are normally mild, the weather can turn nasty. Hunts that were intended to last only a half a day can turn into a much longer ordeal if the wrong circumstances come together.

A few years ago in late October I went into the backcountry of Glacier National Park to photograph mountain goats in their winter coats. It was an unusually mild, snowless October that gave an opportunity to get into an area that was normally unreachable at that time of year.

On the first day of a 2-day trip I was fortunate to obtain some excellent photos of a billy and 2 nannies. That evening I prepared my camp and fell asleep to a glorious red and orange sunset. Because of the clear skies I didn't bother with the tent.

I woke up at 3:00 a.m., cold and wet, to find 3 inches of new heavy snow covering my sleeping bag and ground cloth. I broke camp quickly and headed through the falling snow to a trail crew shack I'd seen on the trip in.

While walking down the trail, I slipped on a patch of ice, dislocating and fracturing my ankle. With the pain, shock, and wet clothes all working against me a severe case of hypothermia set in. My survival gear pulled me through the 3 days I spent on the mountain before the helicopter arrived. Had I not been prepared for the worst, I doubt I'd be here writing about the incident.

If one is prepared for the worst, a state of mental calm can be maintained in adverse conditions. Knowing that the essentials of survival are at hand is comforting; it permits the mind to solve other problems. A tin cup, sterno, candles, granola bars, spare gloves, butane lighter, paper, waterproof matches, and a space blanket are the bare essentials for a survival pack. Don't become complacent and give up taking survival gear on every trip. Ninety-nine times out of 100 it won't be needed. But the 100th time could mean the difference between life and death.

Rob Hazlewood

"This brings up the point concerning the psychology of bow hunting, something I'm almost religious about. To permit an aged, mature bull to be lost because of poor tracking conditions or a misplaced arrow would be unforgivable. Being able to pass up shots at some animals because things aren't just right is the mark of a true sportsman." — *Rob Hazlewood*

Turkey Calls and Elk

Rob Hazlewood is 33 years old and a professional game biologist employed by the U.S. Bureau of Land Management. Rob has hunted elk with both a bow and a gun since he was 17 years old. He has enjoyed consistent success in taking elk, having killed many during his career. Most of his kills have been bulls from spikes on up. Rob now feels efficient enough at elk hunting that he prefers to take only mature bulls. By limiting himself to trophy bulls, a 6x6 or better, Rob is able to enjoy a longer season; to him, hunting only trophy elk is an excuse to be able to hunt the entire season. If he hasn't taken a good bull by the last of the season, he'll take any bull as his family is fond of elk meat.

Rob has become expert in the use of the diaphragm turkey call-grunt tube combination technique of bugling elk. To the best of his knowledge, he was the first to develop the technique of calling cows and calves. Rob is considered an expert in the art of bugling elk and markets under the name Cedar Hill Diaphragm the diaphragm elk call and an instructional tape that describes the use of the combination. His tape is laced with elk hunting tips Rob has learned over the years. Information on his products can be obtained by writing him at 1540 Hayes Dr., Missoula, MT 59802.

I asked Rob to relate one of his most satisfying elk hunts. He chose an exciting take that took place in September 1981 while bowhunting in western Montana. It relates a series of scouting trips and hunts in which Rob attempts to collect a particularly massively-antlered bull.

Rob Hazlewood

I may get a little long-winded but one thing that is important to convey is that a trophy elk is in the eye of the beholder. I recall a story that occurred in Colorado in which a 14-year-old boy killed his first elk, which was a cow. To him that was the biggest trophy in the world. At my stage in life and hunting experience, a trophy elk is a bull which will score at or over 350 Pope and Young Points.

Right off the top I want to say that I believe in pre-season scouting. I also subscribe to the theory that when hunting for elk, especially trophy elk, a lot of different bulls must be looked at to find a good one. In my opinion, understanding the species being hunted is second in importance to pre-season scouting. It is absolutely imperative that the species being hunted be well understood. Read everything available on the animal and learn the species' habits. This information can then to applied to one particular animal in a given set of circumstances. Once a bull is found that meets my standards, I know during the rut that he will be fairly predictable. This study concept applies to hunting any species, be it wild turkeys, mule deer or elk. Learning a species' habits prevents a lot of wheel spinning and reliance on luck to bring success. I believe I can make my own luck.

My story begins in late August 2 weeks in advance of the opening day of archery season. I was scouting an area that I hadn't hunted for 2 or 3 years, but which had always been good for big bulls.

The country is densely timbered, predominantly with Douglas fir and other types of conifers. There are a few dry, south and west facing parks about one to two acres in size, in which grow Idaho fescue grass, a favorite of elk. Late in the fall after the elk have been feeding on green grass all spring and summer, they tend to key on dry parks in which Idaho fescue is growing. This is especially true in Montana and northern Idaho. The first frost kills the grass, curing it at a high protein content and thus providing good nutritional value. Cow elk in particular have the ability to find the best quality forage, which enables them to increase milk production in the spring and enhances fetal growth in the late fall and winter.

It makes sense, then, to locate the types of forages being utilized by the cows during September since the bulls are totally con-

A bull in the high country.

sumed with a desire to be with the cows during the rutting period.
The bulls will follow them there.

Just as a matter of interest, it's interesting to note what the bulls
do following the rut. The big bulls segregate from the cows after
the rut and tend to locate pockets of coarser forage and begin to
feed heavily. This type of forage is often found in the thickest,
densest stands of timber. It also has less nutritional value and
must be consumed in larger quantities than when feeding on
higher grade forages. The cows then are left to utilize the finer
forages containing a higher nutritional value, which results in
healthier calves.

The really big bulls will be with the cows earlier in the rut. They
seem to know where the cows will be. Scouting in August, well
before the rut begins, is important to locate this type of bull.
Again, understanding the species and what the elk will be doing
at a set period in time is essential.

The floor of the basin I was hunting was heavily timbered and
contained several drainage heads in which grew alpine fir. These
drainage areas were moist, providing excellent wallow sites. The
basin and surrounding area (area to me may mean one that is 15
miles square and I'll hunt the entire place) was roadless and could
only be reached by hiking 3 miles. All the ingredients necessary
to hold a good elk population were present. The altitude was
6,500 feet.

I arrived in the basin near the periphery of a small park just before daybreak. Since I had found elk there on past trips, I had a hunch which park the elk would be using and just as it was getting light enough to see, the dark forms of elk became visible in the meadow. They were feeding out of the timber through the meadow towards its uppermost point. As the sun began to rise, lighting the tops of the trees bordering the meadow, I was able to count 42 elk. To my surprise, there was not a bull of any type in the bunch; all were cows and calves.

Suddenly, a large straw-colored bull stepped out of the timber. He stood out like a sore thumb even though he was still in the darkened part of the meadow. His rack was vaguely visible in the dim light; he was worth more study. As the sun rose higher, he worked his way through the meadow toward the cows and slowly drifted into the lighted portion of the meadow. I could now see what an extraordinary bull he was. Even though I'm a game biologist and see lots of bull elk, I was impressed. He was unquestionably the largest bull elk I had ever seen, anywhere. When he put his head back, his antlers stood out at least 2 feet on either side of his body and almost extended past his flanks. I guessed his sword tine to be over 36 inches long. His 5th and 6th points were very long and deeply forked. Now I've taken some big bulls and have seen many nice ones over the years, but this bull was tremendous. He astonished me. There, right in front of me, was the biggest bull elk I'd ever seen. It was an unbelievable feeling.

I watched the bull for 1 hour and 15 minutes, during which time he put his head down to feed only 2 or 3 brief times. He was occupied with watching over his cows. Neither he nor the cows left the meadow the entire period I watched.

While working my way into the meadow, sneaking quietly, I was careful to continually test the wind. My plan was to get in and get out as quickly as possible while learning as much as I could. This was definitely where I would be on opening day. I quietly pulled out of the area.

During the next 2 weeks, I could hardly sleep. Finally, September 5th came around and I was in the basin near the meadow at daybreak. I had studied topo maps and been watching the weather a few days prior to coming in and because of this I decided the elk would be in the timber on the north-facing slope of the basin. I tried to guess as to where the bull would be coming from and my plan was to intercept him on his way to the feeding grounds in the meadow. Once in place and just at the slightest hint of daylight, I cut loose with a bugle — trying to stimulate and locate the bull.

A sizable bull walks right up to a hunter using a bugle in heavy timber.

Depending on the time of the year, bulls have different bugling patterns. At the very beginning of the bugle season in early September, there is a lot of night bugling. This is when the elk establish dominance.

One thing important to understand is the bulls spend the entire summer jockeying for position and rank. In fact, the dominance factor goes back to late winter when the bulls are in small groups. Individuals within these wintering groups get to know each other quite well. As they shed their antlers in April and begin immediately to grow new ones, the lines of dominance become more clearly defined. Dominance isn't something that suddenly comes on with the onset of the rut. The pecking order was been well established by the time the rut begins and the lesser bulls know who the boss is. This makes sense within the concept of energy conservation. A big bull will need all his energy to herd and breed cows, and not to spend it in continual battles with other bulls. Thus, the bigger bulls tend to go into the rut with the largest number of cows. Again, this is a principle of species adaptation.

Later, in the course of the rut, the older, dominant bulls become fanatic and can breed themselves to exhaustion. They then have difficulty holding their harems together and younger bulls then compete for the spoils. In this age group of bulls, there will be less clear lines of dominance and more competitiveness.

Late in the season, the hunter often has snow for tracking purposes. Early-season hunters need greater tracking skill.

But back to my story. Three different bulls answered my initial bugle. Over the years of listening to different bulls bugle, I've developed the skill to judge by voice tone and pitch which bulls are the biggest. A mature bull sounds like he has his head in a 55-gallon drum, grunting like a pig. The sound is deep, heavy and gutteral. Most herd bulls don't bother to bugle very often because they don't want to attract attention to themselves or their cows. Spikes rarely bugle, doing so only if there is no mature breeding bulls in the particular population, and the sound is squeaky and high pitched. Three- or 4-year-old bulls bugle a lot, strutting their stuff so to speak, but are quieted and sneak off when the herd bull steps into the picture.

One of the tricks to bugling is to pressure a bull. Once a bull with cows answers my bugle and begins to move off, the stage is set. Moving himself and his cows away from another bull is a reasonable response from the standpoint of energy conservation. It is more efficient to avoid battle by evasion than confrontation. A second objective is accomplished in that he is less likely to lose his cows to a challenging bull by simply moving them out of the area. Hopefully, the bull in possession of the cows will think I'm a threat if I've bugled convincingly.

I then push the retreating bull, bugling as necessary. Some bulls travel 4 or 5 miles and finally become so irritated they stand to fight. By pressuring the bull, I observe his reactions to determine how good a bull he is. For example, I've pressured bulls into heavy pockets of timber and more or less had them cornered. In this situation, a younger bull, especially one without cows, will quit bugling and sneak out the back door and disappear while a mature trophy bull may stand and accept my challenge.

The 3 bulls that answered my bugle that first morning didn't sound like a real big bull. I felt they were all satellite bulls. I then covered 6 or 7 mountain miles that morning and bugled in 2 small 6x6 bulls, but was unable to locate my big bull. Neither of the 2 bulls had cows, so I knew my bull was holed up somewhere with his harem. It was just a matter of time and I'd locate him!

Mid-day was spent laying low and out of sight. Later, right at dark, I bugled and 5 different bulls answered. One of the 5 sounded deep and throaty and I knew he was my bull. The sound came from near where I had set up that morning, but it was too late to move in on him that day so I pulled back to my camp. The camp was located about 3 miles from the action and I feel that is a good distance to put between myself and the hunting area. It is necessary to camp as far away from the elk concentrations as is reasonable.

That night there was a full moon and the elk were very active. Sleep came hard for me because the elk bugled continually around my camp. Even so, I couldn't locate my big bull over the next 3 days, but I was not to be discouraged. I returned the next weekend and bugled in 3 more bulls, all small ones. As I've mentioned, my philosophy is to be patient and not take a lesser bull. I held true to that conviction. The bulls that responded to my bugle would have scored in the 300 to 325 range, but I wasn't going to settle for an elk that size. I emphasize, however, that it isn't a macho thing with me; it's just that I simply like to hunt the entire season.

After an absence of 2 weeks, with the moon waning, I was back in the basin. It was the 25th of September. By this time I'd lost track of where the bull was. I didn't feel comfortable about his routine because a lot can change in 14 days. I was starting all over again.

It was late afternoon when I arrived at the meadow and I just sat and listened. I heard a small bull bugle, which was immediately followed by the unmistakable roar of my trophy. This picked my spirits up considerably. The tension heightened as he began to move out of a thick stand of Douglas fir and work toward the meadow. He was bugling every few minutes and I was able to trace his movement. I took off, bugling, running toward the direction in which he was moving. When I arrived near him, he was beginning to work himself into a frenzy. He would even

A good rub is all a guy needs to feel good.

answer my mouth bugling.

I worked closer and closer and when within 200 yards of the bull the hair was standing on the back of my neck. He was exactly how I like a bull — totally out of control with rage. If I bugled every 30 seconds or every 2 minutes, he would answer with roars and grunts so loud the trees seemed to shake.

He was just over a small ridge, standing in a shallow drainage. Adequate cover was a problem as the trees were sparse, making it difficult to position myself in the direction he was traveling. His cows were heading up toward a dry fescue meadow to feed and he was following them at a leisurely pace. Just below the meadow was a dense stand of alpine fir through which I thought the elk would travel. As the cows cleared the fir thicket and headed up the hill, I managed, after cautious maneuvering, to position myself in behind the last of the cows and ahead of the bull. The cows were unaware of my presence. The entire time I was stalking him he was either bugling, goring the ground, or raking the trees and brush with his antlers. He was about as worked up as any bull I've seen.

I bugled and the bull answered below me in the middle of the fir thicket. I concealed myself behind a thick, bushy fir tree and in a few moments I could hear the bull's footsteps as he moved toward me. I tested the wind and everything was perfect. But suddenly a straggling cow passed unalerted 15 yards in front of me and the tension was terrific.

The bull unexpectedly changed course slightly to the north and in doing so circled around me and put himself between me and the cows. I thought, "Pretty crafty, you old dude." His move changed the game considerably. Had I remained between him and his cows, he would have run over me. As it was, I would have to lure him that last 20 yards in a direction away from his cows — a considerable problem! The range was so close that parts of him were visible through the thick trees. A patch of hair here and an antler tine there. He hesitated, but continued to answer my bugles aggressively. Every fiber of my body was on super alert. The adrenalin was rushing through me in huge doses! I repeatedly returned the bull's bugles, but he wouldn't come any closer. It was a standoff complicated by fast-approaching darkness.

The bull felt that he had the advantage for 2 reasons: he was uphill and he already had his cows behind him and away from me. Psychologically, the bull was in control. He had no reason to come to me for a fight and as darkness was falling, I knew a hard choice had to be made. I came to full draw and inched by way from behind the cover tree. Very slowly, tiny step by tiny step, I

Not quite hidden, this bull poses serenely behind a small sapling he has just rubbed out.

cleared the tree and as I did so the bull stepped in my direction, exposing himself. I instantly recognized him as the huge bull I had seen on my first scouting trip! Here were were, finally, face to face, eyeball to eyeball, at under 20 yards. He unquestionably was the largest bull elk I had ever seen. But as we stared at each other for those few, fleeting micro-seconds, I knew that it was too dark to make the shot. I made the hardest decision I've ever made and let him turn and walk away.

I know many people will think I'm a fool. Even though I felt very comfortable with the shot, it was too dark. I was uncomfortable with the possibility of losing the bull by not killing him outright. Tracking blood spoor in the dark, or anytime with no snow, can be a touchy situation. This noble bull deserved better.

I never got another chance at that same bull during the remaining archery season.

This brings up a point concerning the psychology of bowhunting, something I'm almost religious about. After killing an 8- or 9-year-old bull, I sit down and contemplate him. My thoughts go something like this: "Why I was just a green kid hunting elk when this guy was a calf. He's been smart and sly enough to survive many winters and escape all sorts of hunters." I really have a lot of respect and admiration for the animal I've harvested. To permit an aged, mature bull to be lost because of poor tracking conditions or misplaced arrows would be unforgivable. Being able to pass shots at good animals because things aren't "just right" is the mark of a true sportsman. It gives one a good feeling.

■■■▬▬■■■▬▬■■

Question: Rob, what is the reason elk bugle? What function does it serve?

Hazlewood: I don't feel we as biologists and researchers are anywhere near understanding the true behavior of the animal, including the reasons they bugle. Big game management on the surface seems simple, but may, in fact, be very complex. For instance, there have been theories presented discussing the thermal cover needs of elk. In reality, every winter day presents a different challenge for the elk. There will be days when the wind blows out of the west and the temperature will be 30 degrees Fahrenheit below zero, while the next day an Arctic air mass may move in from the north and the temperature is 60 degrees below zero. On another day, a chinook may blow into the area, bringing sunny skies and a temperature of 20 degrees Fahrenheit above zero. So thermal cover can't be one patch of timber on a hillside. There may be a series of sites necessary to meet the needs of the animal, depending on annual climatic conditions. The point is, the behavioral needs and expressions of elk are complicated and can't, at the present state of our knowledge, be defined so absolutely.

The meaning of a bull's bugling, I feel, also has to be looked at with an open mind. I have bugled in cows during the rut. This has occurred in areas where there were a number of bugling bulls. I'm not certain of the exact meaning of this. It may demonstrate that there is something to the theory that says that cows are attracted to the bull with the most mature-sounding bugle. I personally suspect this to be a less important function of bugling. If that were the case, the bulls would be a lot more vocal.

Most bulls, in my opinion, use bugling to issue a warning: "Hey, I've got my cows. Stay away!" Possession of cows alone, in the herd bull's mind, establishes his dominance in both the eyes of the cows and satellite bulls. The low gutteral sounds used by the herd bull is for the purpose of talking to his cows. It is part of the herding technique.

Question: What behavioral changes, if any, are elk demonstrating in response to increased hunting pressure and habitat loss?

A hunter's dream, a band of bull elk move into the open but in the shadowed side of the ridge.

Hazlewood: I'm seeing subtle changes in the basic behavior patterns of bulls that have succeeded in reaching the age of 6 to 9 years. They are becoming more like whitetail bucks, being more secretive and hanging in thick pockets of timber. I've been adapting my hunting strategy keeping those observations in mind. I have to get into the densest timber I can find, literally crawling over, under and through downfall and thick timber. I travel at a snail's pace, pushing each branch aside as I go. I have a way to judge a good elk area: if there is no way I could kill an elk in this spot and there is no way I'll ever pack the meat out, I know it's the right spot. Ninety percent of the elk hunters, upon getting into such an area, are immediately overwhelmed and leave. They fight the brush for a few minutes and decide they can't take it. They aren't willing to pay the price. The big bulls that use this "hider strategy" have learned this and therefore they seek out this type of cover.

Question: How do you approach the problem of packing out the elk meat from one of those remote areas you hunt? When reaching the mid to late 30-year-old mark, that becomes a serious question.

Hazlewood: I never wrestle with the problem of getting the

meat out. Doing so would cause me to cease being a good elk hunter. My hunting style never permits me to shoot anything that is easy to get out. When I start to question or wonder about getting the butchered carcass out of the mountains, I know I'm hunting in the right place. I've shot elk before in locations so bad I almost wanted to sit down and cry. Anyone who is a serious trophy hunter can't worry about the problem of getting the meat out of the woods.

After I have the bull on the ground, the problem is approached scientifically, very methodically and unhurriedly. I first tell myself the meat will be taken out! Then I'm in a proper frame of mind. It is, however, critical that you do a good job of boning out the meat. The bones will be discarded at home, so it makes no sense to pack them out. The carcass is opened and skinned quickly. It is then dismembered and the meat removed from the bones.

The procedure for removing meat from the bones is not complicated. Each group of muscles has a point of origin and insertion. These are easily identified by examining the lay of the muscles. By severing these attachments, the bone is easily removed. Proficiency comes with a little practice. After boning, the meat is turned open so the air can cool it. The meat is kept clean by packing it in meat bags. These are then strapped to pack frames and I emphasize that pack frames must be of high quality. Welds have broken under the stress of meat packing. I don't care how steep or rugged the country, the entire project can be done, including packing the head and cape, in four or five trips. I take everything usable out, so the ravens and magpies have a difficult time scrounging a meal once I've finished with the carcass.

Let me tell you a story about a friend named Kyle. He was an off-again and on-again elk hunter and, being a school teacher, of the studious nature, his hunting time consisted of Saturdays and Sundays. I agreed to take him elk hunting as he hadn't been on a hunt for several years and in fact had never killed an elk or seen a dead one. On Saturday, we left early for the mountains where I soon found Kyle's idea of elk hunting was to take off like a jackrabbit and cover as many drainages as possible during the course of the day. He expected to kill an elk and simply drag it out by the antlers, no matter what the distance. I explained that if he killed an elk late Saturday or Sunday 5 drainages over, he'd be at work Monday and guess who would be packing elk. He replied: "Oh, that's no problem. We can just hang it in a tree until next weekend."

We split up and then met back at camp after dark. I had killed a 6x6 earlier that day after we'd parted and I explained to Kyle that we would pack it out in the morning. The next morning, upon

Rob Hazlewood rests from the labors of packing out a trophy taken using his specialized hunting techniques.

reaching the downed elk, I said, "All right, Kyle, now grab him by the horns and let's go." He could barely lift the head. "If you can't drag him, Kyle, just hang him in the tree." He looked up at a big lodgepole pine and then walked around the bull about 4 times while scratching his head. I could see his mind working and he finally replied: "I can see now what you've been trying to tell me all these years. A bull elk is a very large animal."

My point is that people tend to be in a hurry and panic and don't approach the problem with some thought. A successful hunter is anxious to get his trophy home or has to be back for an appointment or for work. At that point, he's already started the mental process of beating himself before he's begun. Trying to work a 70- to 80-pound piece of elk meat through basins and over ridges while in a hurry is crazy.

This past season was the first time I've ever gotten a bull elk out whole. I dragged him with ropes for 7 hours, downhill with little blowdown. Lying on plastic, he slid very nicely on the snow; in fact, sometimes I wondered who was dragging whom. But the key was that I'd thought out a process for getting several hundred pounds of elk meat out in a systematic manner.

Question: When the weather is warm as it often is during the rut, what precautions do you take against meat spoilage?

Hazlewood: There is no reason to lose meat. I try not to shoot animals too late in the evening if possible. The possibility of having a delayed recovery is great; this, of course, can result in spoiled meat. I immediately field dress the carcass and open it as wide as possible. My next step is to quickly skin the animal. Elk hides are built for insulation, so it must be removed as soon as practical. The mountain air in the evenings and at night is quite cool, even in summer, and the boned meat will be chilled by morning.

Question: What role does the wind play while elk hunting?

Hazlewood: One year I remember walking right in on a 6x6 bull and shot him at a range of 22 yards. The bull was in a thick stand of timber and since I was working at close range, the wind was critical. I always carry a small lighter to test wind direction while I'm hunting and when I'm in close to a bull, I've got the lighter working all the time. I flick that lighter more often than a chain smoker and I go through 2 or 3 lighters a season. It is one of the best means of quickly and accurately determining wind direction. If the wind turns unfavorable, I leave immediately. Remember, when elk are in thick timber which limits their vision, they rely heavily on their sense of smell.

Question: What are the 2 most important considerations when hunting elk with a bow?

Hazlewood: I would mention three. The first is successful preseason scouting, which we have already discussed. The second is to pick a spot on the bull before releasing the arrow, and not shoot at the whole bull. The tendency is to shoot at the entire animal when confronted with one the size of a bull elk. A third important consideration is bugling technique. Specifically, don't over-bugle. Two or 3 days of over-bugling will quiet every bull in the country. What constitutes over-bugling? It is strictly a matter of judgment gained with experience or by working with an experienced hunter. Different bulls and different situations might call for changing bugling techniques, including frequency. Be cautious and sensible. Walking down a ridge and bugling like mad is not going to product results.

Question: Rob, would you discuss the turkey call-vacuum hose bugling method you have perfected?

Hazlewood: The diaphragm turkey call coupled with a three-foot length of standard diameter vacuum hose is without doubt the most effective means of mimicking the call of a rutting bull elk on the market today. The grunts, roars and bugles produced using this combination sound exactly like the real thing. It also allows flexibility while bugling. First, using just the diaphragm I can bugle while my hands are free so if the bull hangs up and won't come in the last few yards, I can come to a full draw and attempt to get a clear shot. Second, I can mimic the sounds of cows and calves and as far as I know I am the originator of this technique.

Question: Let's say you walk into a basin and either hear a bull bugle first or get a response to your initial bugle. How do you proceed?

Hazlewood: Generally, a bull doesn't bugle first. Most often I bugle and listen for a response. Most elk hunters, after having a bull answer, are amazed and make the mistake of not setting up. The first thing to do after getting that initial response is to get into a hiding position. If a bull responds, he is in a position to possibly come in — and the maximum distance a bull will respond to the bugle is about one mile. Acoustics, being what they are in mountainous country, make it difficult to determine absolutely where a bull is located. Because of this, I get ready from the outset by put-

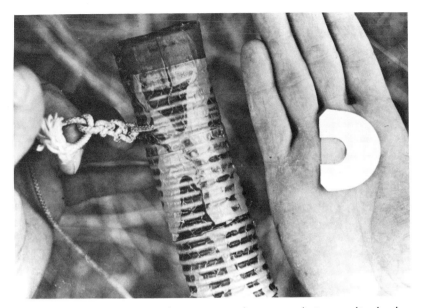

The turkey-call grunt tube combination gives the most realistic-sounding bugles, grunts and yells of any product on the market today.

ting some cover at my back and waiting. Now I've made some advantage for myself. I have time to think and calm down. Where is he? What's going on? What will his next move be? Does he have cows? I generally wait 10 minutes and if no response comes, I bugle again. If he answers and appears to be getting closer, it becomes a waiting game. If his bugle tells me he is in the some place, or moving away, I get up and run toward him. If, say, he's one-half mile away I'll pull up after about a quarter of a mile and set and wait about 15 minutes to catch my breath. I then repeat the process of bugling and listening. When he answers, I try to locate his position more precisely and learn more about his actions. It thus becomes a game of strategy. Once he starts coming, it's a matter of last-minute positioning to place myself in a favorable spot to make a shot. If the bull doesn't come in, I try to determine which way he is moving and position myself to intercept him. During this entire process, I'm very conscious of wind direction. If the wind isn't right, I'll break off my stalk at any time and pull out. If the bull is a good one and I want him, I'll try to figure a way to work around him to get the wind to my advantage. It doesn't bother me to go over 2 ridges and through a basin to get the wind right. If it takes me 2 hours, he will probably remain in nearly the same position.

Question: Do you feel a bow, in the hands of the average archer, is an efficient weapon with which to hunt elk?

Hazlewood: A bow is a very efficient weapon in the hands of a conscientious hunter. I mean by that one who won't take a chance. The critical part about bowhunting elk is having an above-average ability to track wounded game. Persistence while tracking is also important.

Question: Where do you think the next bull that scores in the top 10 Pope and Young scores will be taken?

Hazlewood: There's no doubt in my mind that such a bull will come from Montana, which has adequate security cover — and that is the top priority in producing big bulls. However, Montana is losing more and more secure habitat every year. Logging and the road building associated with logging present formidable problems to elk. I'm personally not anti-logging, but it must be done in a sensible manner with the needs of elk taken into consideration. Leaving every other drainage unlogged and closing logging roads are helpful practices.

Montana has a progressive big game management program and there is considerable cooperation between state and federal game management agencies. This is essential. Many of the men in position to make decisions are into hunting big bulls themselves. Also, right now, Montana's big game population is at high levels and presently there is considerably less hunting pressure than states like Colorado. The future of elk hunting in general is good, although the numbers of big bulls taken will decrease. Even with good management principles, time and so-called progress have a way of eroding the habitat. It is a cumulative problem and we are rapidly approaching the point at which there will be no or at least poor quality trophy elk hunting. Elk hunting in general will continue to be good, but trophy hunting in particular will continue to slide.

Large expanses of isolated country with adequate supplies of cover and forage make optimum elk habitat.

Stan Swartz

"*I know there is a bull at the end of the track. It's my skill against his cunning, my stamina against the winter environment. It is the ultimate challenge.*" — *Stan Swartz*

Hard Work and Iron Sights

Stan Swartz, like myself, is a veterinarian by profession but a woodsman and hunter at heart. He was born in Idaho, but moved to Montana, where he now lives, when just a youngster. Stan started hunting at the age of 19 and has taken many excellent bulls.

At 42, Stan is one of the best conditioned men I have ever seen at any age. His muscles, lean and tight, enable him to use a special kind of elk hunting technique which demands a great deal of stamina and which also is one few men dare try. He is one of the most dedicated elk hunters I've had the pleasure to know and hunt with. Stan hunts only for trophy bulls and only with an iron-sighted rifle. Both choices are just his personal philosophy; he appreciates that cows must be harvested to properly manage herds.

Stan Swartz

The method I use to hunt elk, which I have refined over the years, is to locate a big bull's track in the snow and follow it. I've had more enjoyment and surprises using that procedure than any other technique I've used. It is a one-on-one situation with no chance encounters. It pits my stamina and hunting knowledge against a bull that is mature and has been around for a while.

A real trophy that Stan tracked to his bed.

He's smart and knows the ropes. Over the years, while using the tracking method, I have killed 4 or 5 bulls while they lay in their beds.

Elk nowadays, especially trophy bulls, have acclimated themselves to rough terrain. With few exceptions, elk inhabit the most physically demanding mountains in the Lower 48. Hunting late in November, like I do, complicates this type of hunting because the snow is often thigh deep and the cold penetrating.

Conditioning plays a very important role in not only the enjoyment of an elk hunt, but how successful it will be. There have been a number of times that had I not been in good physical condition I would not have gotten the bull I was after. Had I been slow in reaching a certain place, I would have had no chance for a shot.

A case in point: Hunting with a friend this past fall, I'd spotted a group of elk across a canyon. In the group were three decent 6-point bulls. They were feeding their way across an open hillside and would soon disappear into the bordering timber. I figured it would take about an hour to hike over to the bulls. While trying to reach the bulls, I had to repeatedly stop and let my partner rest. He was really hurting physically. In doing so, we took about 20 minutes longer to reach the elk. We got into position for a shot just in time to see the rear ends of the elk disappearing into the timber;   5 minutes sooner   and we would have had our pick of three bulls.

I start all my hunts well before first light and have worked my way into the back country by dawn. Then I locate a bull's track by moving through the type of rough, isolated country in which I would expect to find a big bull. I usually employ my tracking method of elk hunting in mid or late November, and look for a single track, an animal traveling alone. By this time the bulls have separated from the cows and I can be reasonably certain, after finding a single track, that it was made by a bull. Psychologically, it gives me a mental lift to know that at the end of the track I'm following is a bull, and usually a fairly respectable one.

Once I've found a track I study the prints carefully in an attempt to determine the size of the animal. It is a waste of time and energy to follow a track only to discover the bull is a raghorn, three or four point. I'll examine several of the bull's prints, checking for the roundness of the toes. A sharp-pointed, narrow print, especially when made by the front foot, generally means the animal is an immature bull or one that is not carrying a lot of weight. If the track is more rounded on the outside and wider, the bull probably is a large-bodied one. Some snow conditions make it virtually impossible to tell the size of the bull. Deep, powdery snow won't produce a very well outlined track. In very deep snow, I sometimes even have trouble determining which way the bull is traveling.

A trick I use to determine antler size is to follow the track for one-half mile or so and see what type of terrain the bull goes through. If he goes around small groups of trees which are growing close together, rather than between them, I can surmise the bull's rack is large. Occasionally, a bull will approach a tight fit between 2 trees and the tracks will hesitate, then back up a few steps, and go around.

Several times, I have followed prints which indicated a large animal only to find the sign belonged to an aged bull whose rack was degenerating in both spread and tine length. On other occasions some large prints belong to exceptionally large-bodied 4- or 5-point animals. These aren't the types of bulls I'm looking for. I can say, however, the majority of lone bulls that are roaming the higher, more remote country in deep snow and are leaving big prints, will prove to be a herd bull.

Let me diverge a moment from my story to go over a few points that are critical to a successful elk hunt, no matter what the method followed. The most important factor when hunting elk is wind direction. Inattention to wind direction will ruin a hunt nearly every time. The opportunity to get in close and have a chance at a shot simply won't happen.

In November the weather gets serious. It's highly unpredictable and potentially dangerous.

Some individuals rub their hands and bodies in elk urine found while hunting. I have tried the same and don't feel it does much good. As far as the use of scents in general, it is more important not to reek of a dirty clothes, human-type odor. When hunting out of a camp, for a period of several days, the clothing picks up smoke, cooking, and other assorted camp aromas. These types of odors tend to penetrate clothing and be quite strong. I keep a change of clothes in camp, and my hunting clothes are kept in a plastic bag outside the tent; thus they are relatively free of camp odors.

Sight is an important defense mechanism to elk. In my experience, certain individuals rely on sight defense more than others. I can remember a particular hunt on which I topped a small, brushy ridge and peeked over the other side to peer into a basin that was about one mile away. I immediately spotted a small group of elk and, at the same instant, their heads jerked up as they simultaneously sighted me. The herd quickly took off for parts unknown.

On the other hand, I've, on occasion, been in very close to elk and if the wind was right, had them stand and stare at me. Most often these are cows, calves, and young bulls.

My story took place the third week in November while hunting for a trophy bull. Earlier in the season I had been hunting the Anaconda Pintler Wilderness in south central Montana, having seen several decent bulls but nothing I wanted. I decided to change areas and planned a hunt into the Bitterroot Selway Wilderness. I'm attracted to this wilderness because it is tough, steep, and contains many basins that hunters never reach. Because of the nature of the country, it holds outstanding bull elk. Because the country is so rugged I will only take a superior trophy. It is too difficult and steep to pack meat out of unless the animal is exceptional.

Several miles in the mountains I arrived at the opening of an isolated basin at daybreak. Almost immediately cutting a fresh single track, snow conditions were such that I was able to determine that it was made by a large heavy-bodied bull.

Once a suitable track is found my procedure is to follow very slowly. Subconsciously, out of the corner of my eye, I follow the track while focusing my attention ahead of and around me. I'm careful not to expose myself because once the bull knows he's being followed it's a whole new ball game.

Most often, after cutting a track in the early morning, say before 9 a.m., I'm on the bull by mid-afternoon. Sometimes a bull is in sight as quickly as 20 minutes after picking up his track. Actually, that's one of the points which makes snow tracking so appealling to me. I never know for sure how long it will take me to catch a bull. Accordingly, proceeding very slowly is critical.

After following the bull for 45 minutes, he entered a very thick stand of lodgepole pine. Unfortunately, it was here that the bull jumped out of his bed about 40 yards ahead of me. I just wasn't alert enough to see him first. The trees were too thick to get any kind of a clear shot or even a good look at his rack. It was so dense the bull had difficulty pushing his way out of the timber.

Breaking clear of the lodgepole, the bull ran 400 yards or so and then entered country so thick with blowdown he was forced down to a fast walk. I continued to dog the bull and he, of course, knew he was being followed. After four hours of tracking him, he entered the type of country in which he felt secure and his pace began to slow. I'm sure he felt I was no longer with him.

His trail led into a large basin with a floor of rolling rows of fir-studded ridges with deep canyons between them. The ridges led to the head of the basin where they split into five draws reaching to the top of the ridge. The upper portion of the bowl consisted of broken rocky outcroppings and stunted alpine fir. The altitude near the top of the basin was 7,000 feet. It was ideal big bull habitat.

Nightfall comes early in the mountains this time of year and I was becoming concerned. It was now mid afternoon and my pursuit time would be limited. Electing to sit down on a vantage point where I could see a good portion of the basin I began to glass the area thoroughly. I hoped to visually locate the bull, discontinue tracking, and work the bull directly, saving time.

My luck held. After looking over the ridges only a few minutes I found him. He was in a straight line about three-quarters of a mile away, standing, watching his back trail. Even at the extreme range I could see his huge rack silhouetted against the snow. As he turned his head side to side, ever alert, my eyes were drawn to his antlers. He had symmetry, length of main beam, and was heavy. When he extended his neck forward the tips of his antlers would tickle his rump. He was undoubtedly the nicest bull I've ever seen in all my years of roaming the mountains. He would probably score in the high 380s or low 390s in the Boone and Crockett record book, and was probably a 6- to 9-year-old animal.

There was a fair breeze blowing into and up the basin. The bull had me where he wanted me. There was no way to follow his track without him catching my scent. All the cards were stacked in his favor. There was no percentage, either time or wind-wise, in continuing to follow his track. I studied the situation and decided to drop off the back side of the ridge, out of sight, make a big loop to the bull's left and above him. I'd then have the wind in my favor. The bull probably wouldn't move far as his attitude and body posture, during the 20 minutes I watched him, indicated he felt reasonably safe where he stood. He might even bed where he was and watch his back trail from his vantage point. It was my only chance and, with 3 hours of daylight left, I'd have to hurry.

It took me nearly two and a half hours of hard pushing to make the loop around the outside of the ridge to a position above where I thought the bull would be. It was tough going but it was an all or nothing effort. It was now 4 p.m. and heavily overcast and it would be dark in 40 minutes.

Peeking my head over the ridge, I looked into the basin but didn't see the bull. I started working slowly down the ridge with nearly perfect conditions. The snow was soft, fluffy and very quiet. The wind, as I'd hoped for, hadn't changed direction and was blowing in my face. If the bull had indeed bedded and was watching his back trail, I had a good chance.

I checked my rifle, cleaned off the snow and made certain the barrel wasn't clogged. My rifle is an iron sighted 30-06 shooting a 180-grain bullet. It is like an old friend, dependable and true, having brought down many deer and elk over the years.

Very slowly, I inched my way along the ridge, often getting down on my hands and knees to peer under and through the scrubby tree line pines. I had to see the bull first or it was all over. I was within 50 yards of the small open bench on which I had last seen the bull, and stopped to glass the opening very carefully.

Binoculars, in my estimation, are absolutely necessary to hunt big game. They can be used to evaluate elk at a distance or can be used to identify an ear, antler tine, or a patch of hair while hunting in dense cover at close range. The naked eye simply cannot, in most cases, pick out pieces of an animal standing or bedded in shady, thick brush. Binoculars not only gather available light to brighten the image but also concentrate ones attention on one small portion of brush at a time.

Shortly, I saw what appeared to be a patch of hair about one foot in diameter. Studying the scene intently, I discovered a piece of horn sticking out of the brush. He was bedded where I'd last seen him. He didn't have any idea a human being was within 10 miles; my plan and stalk had been perfect.

There was, though, one major problem. I couldn't see enough of the bull, even at 50 yards, to get a shot at a vital area. I had to somehow change position. The ridge that the bull and I were on was very narrow and steep on each side, making it impossible to drop off either side to position myself for a better shot. This location was so close to the bull that I was afraid to move at all. One snapped twig or one heavy breath and it was all over.

Because of the closing darkness, the only option was to attempt to somehow change my position slightly and get a better view of the bull, and at 50 yards that is no easy trick.

I carefully lowered myself into a crawling position and slowly bellied ahead 10 yards through to snow to reach a small, bushy pine. This accomplished 2 things. The tree could be used for a gun rest and a small patch of the elk's neck could be seen clearly. Even at 40 yards, it wasn't much of a target but it would have to do. The bull was pointing away and looking down the basin, still totally unaware of my presence.

Let me say that I don't like neck shots. There is so little vital area as compared to the chest cavity. I've seen several neck-shot animals run off and never be recovered. Nevertheless, it appeared a neck shot would be my only option. My actions in the next few seconds would decide success or failure. It would be just a matter of moments until an errant gust of wind or the bull's sixth sense would give me away. I was too close! Wracking my brain, I pulled on all my years of experience to choose the best course of action.

A soft whistle or breaking a twig would cause the bull to stand, but I ruled that out. Too many times, at close range, I've had bulls explode out of their beds at the slightest noise or motion. They offered no shot and were gone in a flash. With that in mind, I went for the neck shot. I rested the rifle on a tree branch, collected myself as best I could, sighted carefully on the area of the neck where I judged the spine to be — and squeezed off a shot. What happened next was almost unbelievable. The bull instantly, in a huge spasmodic lurch, flipped to its left and turned upside down on its back. His neck and antlers extended straight away from his body, with the antlers impaled in the snow. The bull's front legs were rigid, extending straight into the sky. In a few seconds he relaxed, fell over on his side and was motionless.

I had a good idea from watching the bull through binoculars how large his rack was, but as I stood up and walked toward the bull I saw he was the kind of elk I'd been after for years. He was the "biggie." His left antler had 8 large points and the right antler had 7 equally large points. I began to relax and pat myself on the back for planning a good stalk and making a good shot. Then, just as I got to within a few steps of the bull, to my utter consternation and amazement, he jumped to his feet, whirled and instantly disappeared around the curve of the ridge. It happened so fast I didn't have time to raise my gun.

My first thought was, "The bull went down fast and hard, so the shot must have been well placed." It would be just a matter of time until I found him. Twenty minutes passed while I glassed the country into which he'd run. Unable to see the bull, I started on his track and noted he was bleeding but not badly. While tracking him, I was making mental notes concerning my situation. I faced some hard decisions. It would be pitch dark in less than 15 minutes and I was 9 miles from my truck. I had with me my usual emergency gear in a small daypack. The pack contained a two-day food supply, flashlight, firestarter, and a small canvas tarp. I decided to track the bull with the remaining light and go from there.

I checked the bull's gait to determine the severity of his wound. He wasn't limping or dragging any of his limbs and moved strongly. He dropped off the ridge where I'd shot him, jumping blowdowns as he went, clear to the bottom and started up the other side. This was a bad sign as hard-hit elk usually travel down or at best parallel to the mountain slope and avoid downfall where possible. I began to feel that the bull wasn't badly wounded. Then, after about 15 minutes of tracking, I caught a glimpse of his back and rear quarters as he broke out of a patch of timber ahead of me, but darkness forced me to give up for the day.

At this point I still felt optimistic that I would get the bull. I should be able to pick up his track in the morning and continue to push him, I thought. I flagged, with a florescent surveyor's tape, the point where I last saw the bull and walked out to my truck.

The next morning at daybreak I was collecting the marking flag and again took up the bull's track. I followed him for 5 hours before finding where he'd bedded down. He'd chosen his bedding site very carefully. It was in a small patch of short, thickly-branched fir trees. The depth of vision into the trees was almost nil. He, as smart old bulls do, had bedded on the far side of the thicket. It would have been impossible for me to get through the trees undetected. The bedding site was abandoned when I found it, but there was some blood, but not much, in the bed.

Continuing on the bull's track the rest of the day, I discovered a small grassy park about dark where he'd fed and passed manure. The elk had used both front feet to paw down through the snow and it appeared he was getting stronger and re-establishing normal routines. Even so, throughout the day I had discovered several neck and shoulder-high branches smeared with blood and I became concerned that the bullet wound had damaged the bull's throat or esophagus, which would prevent him from feeding.

At any rate, I covered 10 miles while following the bull on that second day, and I never saw him. At dark I again flagged his track, left and walked out to my truck.

The next day, the third of tracking, I was at my flag at dawn. Picking up the track, I traveled about 300 yards down a ridge, and noticed that across a small basin was a patch of short, bushy trees similar to the bedding site the bull had chosen the previous day. Before totally exposing myself, I stopped to glass the patch of bushy trees. Sure enough, my hunch was right! Just on the back edge of the trees I saw a piece of his antler. If I continued on his track, he would quickly spot me. I attempted another looping maneuver to again move around, behind and above the bedded bull. The country was noiser and brushier than I expected, however, and the bull jumped and ran when I was about 20 yards from him. His horns and the top line of his back were all that I could see as he disappeared.

I followed him for another 4 hours until dark and never saw him again that day. Once again, I flagged his track and walked to my truck.

It was now apparent that the bull was recovering rapidly from his wound. It was as though I was tracking a bull that had never been shot. He was navigating grades that were difficult for me to climb and I now confidently assumed there had been no permanent damage.

On day four I was at my flag at daylight, ready to try again. The bull was heading into an entirely new area and a different type of country. He was still in the high country, but was heading down toward civilization and a roaded area that had been logged.

Following his track, I found two different bedding sites and heard him ahead of me once. I was starting to catch him. About this same time a dog started barking and I heard a chainsaw running. I realized I was only 400 yards from a logging road and someone was cutting firewood in a clearcut ahead. I feared that I might drive the bull to the wood-cutting party and he'd be shot. I followed him into the opening where he hit the logging road, walked along it for a short distance and then dropped off the downside to avoid the woodcutters. By then nightfall was closing in, so for the fourth time I flagged his trail and walked out.

That night it snowed very hard and I was unable to locate the bull's track the next morning. I crisscrossed through the timber for some distance out from my flag, but never was able to locate any sign. My trophy escaped after 4 days of tracking covering a distance of about 35 miles. In the 20-odd years I've been hunting elk, I have shot 2 bulls that have dropped at my shot and got up and escaped; this huge trophy was one of them. The other bull was a similar situation, a neck shot.

As a parting comment, I'd say of all the animals I've hunted the trophy bull elk is the top big game animal in North America. I respect a mature bull's intelligence and his physical attributes.

▄▄

Question: Stan, hunting big game in the West with an unscoped rifle is almost unheard of nowadays. Why do you hunt with iron sights?

Swartz: It's just a personal philosophy. I guess I'm just a traditionalist, having been trained to hunt with iron sights and having hunted with them all my life. I do admit that rifle scopes offer some advantages.

I hunt thick, brushy type country and feel I can get on an animal quicker with open sights than with a scope-sighted rifle. Through the years I've not had occasion to pass a shot or miss shots because of not having a scope on my rifle. The tracking and stalking type of hunting I do goes hand-in-glove with iron sights. It's rare that I take a shot over 100 yards.

My father told me a story years ago. He was hunting elk in the Idaho portion of the Selway Bitterroot Wilderness and was using a scope-sighted rifle. He was working a group of elk when a heavy mountain snowstorm moved in and obliberated the scene. His scope was also obliberated by the snow flakes.

Question: What are the two most important considerations when hunting trophy elk with a rifle?

Swartz: That's an easy question for me to answer. In a nutshell, paying attention to wind direction and having one's body in good physical condition. Failure to watch and take into account the wind is probably the   number 1   reason elk hunters fail. That is, providing the hunter can get into elk country.

Question: Do you think there are currently good numbers of large bulls to be had, or is the trophy population decreasing?

Swartz: The chance of bagging a heavy 6-point bull or better is getting slimmer every year. Access to isolated back country is increasing because of roading activities. Also, the number of hunters increases every year as the amount of habitat decreases. As a result, in most cases the bulls don't have time to attain trophy size.

Twenty years ago I could go out hunting using my tracking technique and see 6 or 7 excellent 6-point or better bulls during

Once an elk is down the real work begins.

the season. In the last 8 to 10 years, I've come to feel fortunate to track down 1 real trophy. I'm not seeing the bulls in the numbers I used to. As far as numbers of elk, I'm seeing about the same as I have over the past 20 years. However, if the loss of critical winter range due to development continues at the present rate there will be a general, across-the-board decline in elk numbers.

Question: What do you think the future of elk hunting in the Northern Rockies will be?

Swartz: I'm concerned about the destruction of winter range. I'm referring specifically to subdivision developments and other human uses of winter range. These areas are at lower elevations, can be roaded easily, and offer attractive scenery. I've seen a tremendous amount of winter range gobbled up for residences. Summer range is not a factor, but the habitat will support only the number of elk the winter range can carry.

I think we'll always have elk hunting. However, I can foresee the possibility of a 7-day permit only season. Unless things change, the days of going downtown and buying an elk tag at will and then going hunting are going to be a thing of the past. I predict we will see this happen in 15 to 20 years.

This is tremendous elk country and very typical of the lodgepole pine forests found throughout much of the Northern Rockies.

A bull elk feels very secure in the dense cover of a lodgepole pine forest.

Greg Munther

"A word biologists have coined to describe elk habitat is 'micro-site.' A good understanding of micro-site habitat selection by elk is necessary to locate them consistently, and that is the name of the game is finding elk." — Greg Munther

Consistently successful elk hunters do. A word biologists have coined to describe elk habitat is "micro-site." A good understanding of micro-site habitat selection by elk is necessary to locate them consistently, and that is the name of the game in finding elk. Elk hunters in general aren't aware of these areas and to them the woods are just the woods. By randomly walking through the forests, hunters spend about 10 percent of their hunting time in the right micro-site areas. Ninety percent of their hunting time is spent combing areas which have no elk or places which have been vacated.

I've hunted with friends where we have split up but were more or less hunting the same country. I will have been fortunate enough to see maybe a half a dozen bands of elk and my hunting partner will see only one. It doesn't mean he is doing anything wrong; it's just a matter of hunting in the wrong spots.

Every minute of the day while I'm hunting, I'm thinking about what the elk are doing and the type of habitat they are looking for. Preferred micro-sites continually change, depending on climatic conditions, seasons and the time of day. Many hours spent observing elk are necessary to develop the skills to locate and understand micro-sites.

For example, when the weather is mild or hot elk spend a lot of time in wet, boggy areas but if, for a few nights, a hard frost covers the ground the elk will move up on the drier sidehills. If a hunter were to hunt these bottom frost pockets even though the ground is covered with tracks, he'd be wasting his time. He would be hunting the area a few days to a week late.

I recall another example of the micro-site principle. I'd been watching a group of elk that were spending the daytime hours bedded high on a ridge, but at night would drop 1,000 feet in elevation to feed in the sagebrush. In the predawn hours, they would would travel single file back to their bedding sites on the ridgetop. I watched the elk follow this pattern ritualistically for three days. The elk there are still following a similar routine and as a result I've killed a trophy bull from that herd and could probably kill others in the future. The point I'm trying to make is if I were to hunt elk in the sagebrush feeding area just after dawn, I'd see no elk. The proper place would be an ambush site along the return route to the ridge.

I have discovered that the elk in this band will shift their bedding sites slightly from year to year, moving up or down the ridge. I now know this particular country so well it is not difficult to relocate the elk each season because their basic pattern of bedding, feeding, times and routes remains nearly unchanged. The only problems that might arise to radically alter their activity would be a severe weather change or increased hunting pressure.

I have difficulty picking out one hunt, however, that I've enjoyed more than another so I'll relate two or three of my favorites:

My very first elk hunt, which actually started out as a goat hunt, occurred in Idaho near the town of Salmon. I was 18 years old and the proud possessor of a recurve bow and a quiver that carried only 5 arrows. On the way up the mountain I shot 2 arrows at porcupines so after reaching the top, ready to hunt goats, I had three arrows left. As I was looking for the goats, an elk bugled. I was a little surprised as the top of the ridge was typical goat country, windswept and rocky. Well, as fate would have it, the elk season was open and I just happened to have my first class, homemade bamboo elk bugle with me. I bugled at the bull and he answered.

Well, the bull and I bugled back and forth a few times and to my surprise his outline appeared, at distance of about 60 yards, as he walked toward me through a rocky saddle in the ridge. He hesitated and started raking the stunted trees with his antlers. As I stood with dropped jaw, he caught my scent and took off down the mountain. I then proceeded to sling arrows at goats for the remainder of the day, having great fun clanging and breaking them in the rocks. At that tender age, I thought it had been a pretty fair day.

A new supply of arrows in hand, I returned the next weekend to search again for goats and perhaps for the bull. All week long was spent thinking about the bull and what to do if I relocated him. I wanted very badly to get a second chance at that elk.

I arrived roaring to go and began climbing into the rocks in the general area where the bull had been the previous week. Hunching down in the brush, I bugled. A novice, I wasn't too surprised when the bull answered. In over a week he hadn't moved out the of the area. I struck a match to test the wind and felt cocky as the smoke drifted off in a favorable direction.

The bull bugled a couple of more times as he moved toward me. I ran across the mountain in an effort to cut the distance between us, hid myself behind a down log, and waited. Sure enough, in a few minutes he walked directly in front of me, 30 yards away. There were no cows — the bull was alone. He never looked my way as I rose, drew back the old recurve and shot. Excited, I hit the bull too far back and high but was lucky enough to cut the aorta, which is the major artery leaving the heart.

Although hard hit, the bull was so charged with adrenalin that he just moved a step or two and continued to bugle. Paying little attention to the arrow, he then reached down and bit off a mouthful of grass, slowly trotted off a fair distance and fell over dead. Now that was pretty heavy stuff for a green kid and I was jumping up and down kicking my heels. Looking back on it now, I realize I didn't know much about hunting elk and was just lucky enough to have had things go my way.

Thinking about that bull brings to mind an interesting point. I've shot many deer and elk in the years since with arrows and have had several of them, even though mortally wounded, act completely oblivious. I'm convinced there is very little discomfort experienced by these animals until their lungs become congested or hemorrhaging becomes severe enough to cause weakness. I've discussed the subject with M.D.s and they indicated there would be very little pain with a lung shot. My observations are that animals in general have a high tolerance to pain. Many arrow-shot animals, if not pushed, do not appear to feel threatened. They move off a short distance, begin to feel sick or faint, lay down and die.

As the years rolled along I became more interested in taking only mature, herd-type bulls. I began to spend more time hunting in the type of remote country where this kind of bull can be found. My technique is to move fast, almost at a dogtrot, and cover a lot of country. As I move along, my eyes are always scanning the ground and my mind is noting the concentration and direction of the tracks, habitat types and the topography. In September, during the rut, I don't have the hindrance of snow and I can put in many miles, often covering 15 or more in a day. Many of my bowhunting friends laugh at my fast pace and ridicule my noise, claiming I spook game.

The motive behind this method of hunting is to locate active micro-sites. The country in between, in my opinion, should be traversed as quickly as possible. Time is wasted spending it in areas where there are no elk. Once I've located elk, I proceed very slowly and assess the situation. Aware of the wind direction, I'll check for wallows, rubs, and fresh tracks in an attempt to determine what classes of elk I'm dealing with and how fresh the sign is.

Incidentally, for the past season or two I've started keeping written records of my hunts and observations on 3-by-5 cards. In order to make myself a more skilled hunter, I make notes of shot distances, dates and locations of kills, and other pertinent information.

I've also found I have developed a preference to hunt alone. Although I enjoy companionship, I realized that even when I hunt with someone else we always split up and meet back at camp after dark. When I hunt elk, I don't compromise; I turn into an animal. I really do! I don't care to be distracted about thoughts of home, what a hunting companion might be doing, or any other interests. I clear out my mind to concentrate totally on elk.

With the wrong hunting partner, there is always compromise such as his being late getting out of camp, being too tired to go one more ridge, or worried about how we're going to pack out the meat. A wise hunter will always select a partner who has a weak mind and enjoys packing elk meat on his back, the saying goes. I agree. I have a few very close hunting companions and it is always understood that we split up and hunt separate directions during the day. A good partner understands that we both then have the freedom to make adjustments and we never have to feel guilty about dragging a person where he may not want to go.

In late September of 1982, I took my latest trophy bull while hunting in west-central Montana. I was working a series of ridges at altitudes varying from 6,500 to 7,000 feet, which had lodgepole pine on the north slopes and Douglas fir interspersed with fescue parks on the south slopes. There were flat benches here and there that the elk used as bedding sites. Having made scouting trips onto these ridges, I'd heard several bulls bugling near the top. One in particular sounded good; he stood out from the rest. He didn't have the high pitched squeal of an immature bull, but the deep, Hereford bull-like bellow of a herd bull.

I decided to play this group of elk by ear. Most of my hunts work out that way. There is no particular master plan once I've into elk. I play each situation moment for moment, depending on the turn of events. I call it "adaptive strategy."

Although I realize it sometimes works for others, I don't believe in a lot of bugling. I've found out over the years that too many things can go wrong. Bugling doesn't work well with a single hunter, at least not with me. Elk responding to the bugling are zeroed in on me, directly, more or less pinning me down. My options and ability to make adjustments involving changes of position are limited. If two hunters are involved, with one not bugling and laying in ambush as the bull moves in, bugling works better. Bugling is more or less a method of locating bulls for me. However, once in a while a bull becomes so hot and reckless I will attempt to bugle him in for a shot.

I have another weird strategy that sometimes works. On occasion I've inadvertently jumped elk at close range and have taken off after them on the run. I'll jump blowdown, dodge trees, and run after the herd as fast as possible. Sometimes only half the herd will be alerted, having keyed in on me originally, but if con-

Elk recline and rest in heavy timber during the day and a careful stalk could be possible.

ditions are right I can run into the group and catch animals that are confused.

Anyway, I had a feeling that the herd bull was hanging high in the timber with his cows until late in the evening and then moving down. I didn't bugle at all, not wanting to attract attention to myself or discourage their feeding movements. I glanced at the piece of unwaxed dental floss tied to my bow. It was shredded on the end from use and was very sensitive to wind direction. A gentle breeze was blowing down the ridge; everything was set.

The importance of wind direction can't be over-emphasized. It should be worked constantly. If the wind changes to an unfavorable direction while I'm stalking a bull, I leave the area or at least back off and try another approach route.

I very cautiously worked my way up the ridge, following the general direction of a well-used elk trail I'd found on a flat, lightly-timbered ridge. The trail led through a heavy stand of doghair lodgepole pine where I suddenly spotted the animals. They stood unalarmed, probably having just risen out of their beds. By this time it was getting late, about one hour before dark. The situation was such that any kind of stalk was out of the question. I was too close and there were too many eyes and ears alert for danger. The herd would eventually begin to move down the trail I had been following and perhaps offer a chance for a shot. The dental floss showed the wind remained favorable and I watched the herd for nearly an hour. The bull was very good and I wanted him badly. But he was in no hurry to move out, being contented for the moment to amble quietly among his cows and nuzzle them occasionally.

All I could do was wait for the lead cow to make her move toward the feeding area. Minute after minute passed and the evening shadows lengthened. The herd would begin to stir soon, but would it be too dark?

With about 10 minutes of daylight to spare the herd began to travel. Single file, led by an old cow, they walked by me one at a time. I dared hardly to breathe as some of the cows passed me as close as 10 yards. A few of the cows spooked as they filed past me down the trail, placing themselves in a downwind position. Fortunately, they trotted down the trail in the original line of travel. The bull apparently wasn't unduly alarmed as there wasn't a wild, panicked scattering.

The bull, wanting to maintain contact with his cows, broke into a fast walk. I let him pass me to a point about 15 yards down the trail. His attention was riveted on the cows, so I stepped clear, drew and released an arrow. The shaft quartered into his flank high and behind the ribs. I was immediately disappointed in the shot, thinking I had hit the bull too far back.

I have firm convictions about how to proceed after arrowing a critter, especially when dealing with an animal the size of an elk. I allow lots and lots of time to elapse before starting to track. The amount of time depends on where the animal is hit. A liver-shot animal would be handled differently than a lung-shot animal.

Over the years I've made some bad shots with arrows, but have lost   only 1 animal that was wounded with what I consider a mortal shot. Being very inexperienced at the time, I believe now that this loss could have been prevented if my present knowledge had been applied to the situation. I'm convinced that too-early pursuit is a major cause of losing wounded animals. For instance, waiting a minimum of 8 hours before beginning to track a gut-shot elk is not unreasonable.

The bull trotted off out of sight down the ridge and stopped about 200 yards away, where I could hear him grunting and bellowing. Not even bothering to walk the few yards to check the ground where the bull had been standing when hit, I knew that he had a mortal wound and checking for blood would have accomplished nothing. I flagged my position and walked to my truck.

The next morning I returned with my packboard and found the bull stone dead near the same location I'd last heard him grunt. The arrow, after all, had penetrated the lungs from behind.

I may be criticized for leaving a fatally-wounded animal such a long length of time in warm September weather, but the next morning after quickly skinning, butchering and boning the bull, only 10 pounds or so of meat was lost even though the bull probably died shortly after I left the previous evening. Skinning and boning immediately were keys to saving the meat.

My 1981 season was a tough one. The weather was unusually hot and for some reason the elk were reclusive. I couldn't find them in any of my favorite spots. Finally, in desperation, I tried a totally new area.

I hiked several miles into the mountains and was suffering through a long, very unproductive day. Late in the morning, while walking along a high, dry lodgepole ridge where the habitat wasn't what I had expected, I was thinking about turning back. I was completely bummed out, having seen very little sign, no fresh tracks, and feeling that I had wasted an entire morning. I sat down and bugled one final time in an attempt to save my hunt.

A glimmer of hope returned when a bull unexpectedly answered from a long distance away, near the bottom of the adjacent drainage. Checking the wind, I dropped off the ridge toward the bull. I assumed he would soon be moving out of the creek bottom and up the opposite ridge to spend the remainder of the day. My plan was to intercept him somewhere along the route and make a stalk.

As I neared the bottom of the ridge and was almost to the creek, I still hadn't caught sight of the bull — or any other elk, for that matter. Not wanting to give away my presence by bugling, I preferred to wait and see how things developed. I worked my way into the timber along the creek and heard the bull bugle as he moved up the opposite ridge about 150 yards above me and just out of sight through the trees. I moved up the ridge as quickly as possible trying to position myself in the direction the bull seemed to be moving and hunkered down behind a large granite boulder. I figured the bull would pass near the boulder, which was located on a small, flat bench.

In a few minutes, a cow cleared the timber about 70 yards away. The bull wasn't alone! Sometimes events go right and as luck would have it, the cow fed to within 25 yards of my boulder. I thought maybe, just maybe, the bull would follow her. Again my luck was true. Suddenly I saw antlers bobbing through the trees and drifting in the direction the cow had taken. My first look at the bull was exciting — he would score over 300 Pope and Young points.

The bull then did a very curious thing. In his path, about 35 yards from my hiding place, was a medium-sized tree that had blown over. It leaned at a high oblique angle to the ground. The bull chose to go under the blowdown rather than around it. Moving forward to pass under the log, he lowered his head and tilted his antlers sideways so they would clear. I realized that the bull's attention would be focused for a brief second on negotiating the blowdown. Accordingly, I chose the precise moment his antlers were just beginning to clear the log to draw my bow. He immediately saw me, but was in an awkward position. He could neither move left or right effectively and rather than backing up, he stepped forward and cleared the blowdown. The instant he was clear of the downed tree, I released my arrow and got deep penetration into the chest cavity and severed the aorta. The bull trotted off brisky for about 60 yards, stopped and began to wobble. Soon, he fell over dead.

This was one of those hunts on which, once the game was located, everything went perfectly. It was a satisfying hunt for me. The bull ended up scoring 318 Pope and Young points.

Question: Greg, do you wear camouflage clothing when hunting?

Munther: No, I usually don't. I believe in quiet clothing and haven't seen durable camo cloth that was quiet. I wear soft flannel or cotton shirts that are dull green or brown plaids. My pants are made of soft cotton-polyester mix material. I do dab a little camo make-up on my face to take the sheen off my nose, cheeks and forehead.

As a general rule camo clothing isn't that important as long as good hunting principles are followed and clothing isn't in high contrast with surrounding vegetation.

Question: You describe letting elk pass by and selecting a shot from behind. Discuss your feelings about that.

Munther: I don't like to have elk looking at me or at least not be in a position to do so when I draw and shoot. Once slightly past me, their vision isn't such an acute problem. Such shots don't always work well with every species. Some, such as antelope and bighorn sheep, have very good peripheral vision. Also, elk don't seem to startle as easily from behind. To prevent any chance of alarming the elk, I make sure the wheels of my bow are well lubricated and my arrow rest is soundproofed. Most of my shots are at close range and these are important considerations.

Lastly, I like the shooting angle from slightly behind. An arrow can be placed in behind the ribs instead of risking hitting the shoulder blade. Frontal shots offer poor opportunities for a killing shot and result in wounded animals.

Question: Do you prefer to shoot a compound bow?

Munther: I'm presently retiring my compound and I'm in transition back to a recurve. The image of the sport of bowhunting is getting tarnished and garbaged by all the gadgetry and I want to divorce myself from the trend. The era of the slob archer may be at hand. The sport has changed radically in the past several years. Twenty years ago there was a small nucleus of hard-core archers in my hometown of Idaho Falls. They were dedicated to the sport in its purist form. There were probably 10 serious archers in the entire town. I remember 1 year, about 1962, putting in for and getting a permit to take goat with a bow. There were a total of 10 permits to be issued for 1 small area and I hurriedly did my preseason scouting since I was anxious to collect a goat before the small herd was spooked by competing archers. I needn't have worried. I got a goat and after the season ended I went to the Fish and Game office to check on the sizes and numbers of goats taken by other bowhunters. To my surprise, not a single other bowhunter had even applied for a permit. Today hundreds apply and the sport has indeed changed.

Question: You previously mentioned your feelings concerning how to proceed after hitting big game with an arrow. Would you elaborate?

Munther: If there is one thing to impress upon bowhunters, it is the importance of following proper procedures after arrowing a deer or elk — particularly if the hit is poor. Lost game only gives the sport of archery hunting a bad name. Sooner or later we all talk to an irate gun hunter who has killed an elk only to find a broadhead buried in its body. It leaves him wondering how many others were shot, died and were not recovered.

I personally feel there are a lot of nonfatal arrow wounds inflicted on big game, with most of the animals fully recovering. I once took a healthy 4-point mule deer and observed the buck some time before killing it. Upon skinning the   I found 2 X-shaped scars in the hide. One was near the brisket and the other was over the shoulders, which led me to deduce the deer had been shot from either above or below with the arrow completely penetrating the muscular portion of its shoulder from top to bottom. The deer was fat and in good condition, having suffered no lasting effects from the arrow wound.

It is just not necessary to lose animals that are hit in a vital spot — and vital spots mean the lungs, spine, major vessels, or the abdomen. Let me give you a couple of examples. Three years ago I gutshot a mule deer. It was a bad shot, pure and simple, but I happened to be hunting in very open country and had an opportunity to watch the deer's reaction for a considerable period of time.

The deer stood in one spot for 5 hours without moving, after which it laid down. Now, if I had attempted to track the deer in 30 minutes or 2 hours I would have pushed it out of the country and could very well have lost it. I let the deer lay for an additional hour until 7 p.m. that evening. With impending darkness, I decided to make my move. I crawled within 15 yards of the deer and placed a second arrow into its lungs. It jumped up and ran about 100 yards before it died, acting as if it had never been hit. Remember, this was a deer. Elk are much stronger. It is difficult to wait too long to begin tracking, especially with an animal shot in the abdomen. Interestingly, when I field dressed the deer I discovered the arrow had not penetrated the liver or kidneys but had lacerated the small intestine, spilling its contents into the abdominal cavity. The deer would have eventually died of shock and peritonitis, which is infection in the abdominal cavity.

A lung shot presents a different situation. The lungs are a very vascular organ and massive hemorrhage can be expected when they are penetrated by a sharp broadhead. Therefore, the waiting time prior to tracking the animal can be reduced significantly. This past season I hit a very nice whitetail buck square in the chest but penetrated only one lung. I waited a full hour before beginning to track him, knowing I had a good hit. The blood trail was adequate to follow and as I approached the buck he died.

I've taken 4 bears with a bow and have yet to find the first drop of blood. The fatty tissues seal around the arrow and the dense fur coat soaks up any blood that does leak out of the wound, making a blood trail nearly nonexistent. After hitting a bear I try to project his course by line of sight as long as possible. This gives me at least a place to start tracking. Fortunately, I have not made a bad shot on a bear and consequently they haven't traveled far. Someday I may and I expect difficult tracking. Anyway, bears should not be pushed too soon after a shot because of scant blood trails and difficult tracking conditions in the spring. The rule of thumb about waiting half to three-quarters of an hour is fine for a lung shot, but not for less vital hits. Jumping a wounded animal after it has had time for the blood to clot will mean difficult tracking, long distances to travel and increased chances of losing the animal.

Question: You made the statement that elk are not as difficult to hunt as other species. Why?

Munther: The secret is knowing elk and having a good feel for how they behave. I give a lot more credit to the evasive habits of whitetail bucks than I do elk. When elk aren't pursued they aren't very wary, make a lot of noise carrying out their daily routines and they don't react to some noises in a hypersensitive manner. These are personal opinions and I know that all elk hunters won't agree with me.

Also, I hunt a lot with maps. I study Forest Service maps and topographical maps to locate roadless areas, to check elevations, and determine vegetative habitat types. Elk are so predictable in their habits and habitat preferences I can get a good idea of where they may be even before hunting in country I've never seen before. Anyone can follow the same procedures and locate good elk areas. All that is necessary is a little study time.

Question: You are currently involved in helping set guidelines for the development of new logging roads and the closure of some old ones on the Lolo National Forest. Would you discuss those plans?

Munther: Our intent is to develop a future travel plan for the Lolo Forest based on recent research and studies which have shed light on the effects open logging roads have on elk and their habits. In the past, a lot of road building followed no particular plan with regard to elk or their habitat needs. New road construction and road closure policies were decided without as much forethought or logic as our intensive management now dictates. The whims of foresters usually decided road density and numbers.

One surprising point that came to light in one study was that constant traffic such as that found on a freeway doesn't affect elk as much as an occasional jeep moving along a logging road. The steady flow of fast moving, nonstop traffic had little effect, whereas the occasional vehicle represented out-of-the-ordinary activity to the elk.

Presently on the Lolo Forest, we would like to maintain the numbers and miles of usable roads now in existence. There will be a lot more roads built to serve the needs of forest management, but by concurrently closing other roads the total number of open roads can remain at the same level as today. We feel this policy is a must if we are to maintain the elk hunting opportunities we now have.

The Lolo's roading plan was designed around consideration to maintain productivity. High quality elk habitat will have no more than one mile of road per open section (a section of land being one square mile). We have begun closing existing roads in prime elk habitat which currently have a higher road density. We are, as forest managers, making an attempt to satisfy the logging interests without sacrificing good elk habitat. This policy sometimes conflicts with those people who feel all roads should be open for their use.

We have found there is better public acceptance of road closures when we close new roads as soon as logging is completed. After a road has been used for a time by wood gatherers and hunters, there is resistance to closures. Early closure of roads has resulted in less vandalism and gate destruction and the public in general seems to be accepting the idea of road closures better than in years past. Hopefully the day will come when we can save the expense of gates if hunters and other recreationists will respect a simple closure sign.

Red Simpson

"Drink and enjoy every mountain vista. Appreciate every elk hunt as if it were your last." — *Red Simpson*

An Outfitter's Touch

Red Simpson has been an outfitter and guide for 30 years. He is a native of Ohio, but came to Montana originally to study forestry at the University of Montana. While tudying in the late 1950s, Red began wrangling for an outfitter part-time in order to supplement his income. He became hooked on the idea of packing and riding broncs into the wild places of Montana, but in a few years tired of working for the other man and bought his own outfit in the early 1960s.

For a while, Red ran his string and went to school at the same time, but after graduation he turned his horse toward the mountains and never looked back. "There are presently in the neighborhood of 600 outfitters in Montana with only a handful that support themselves and their families solely from the income derived from the outfitting business," Red says.

Red has modified his philosophy and operation to cater to those who sincerely want to enjoy a remote, wilderness, horsepacking experience. He operates all summer taking guests into the mountains to fish, sightsee or just relax. All pursuits are in ample supply as Red's territories are the Bob Marshall Wilderness and the Selway-Bitterroot Wilderness, both of which contain spectacular terrain. It is in such places that a person can cleanse his soul: solitude, clear, clean air and magnificent mountain vistas bring a person back to earth, to reality.

During the summer, Red, his wranglers, and assorted guests

make 15 separate trips covering about 100 miles each. Trips are limited to 8 to 10 people, preferably family groups or other individuals interested in the type of trip in which he specializes. He attempts to provide a total wilderness experience by interpreting the country for his guests and making them feel at home.

Red puts on an additional 500 miles, give or take a few dozen, during the hunting season for a total of 2,000-plus miles per year riding a horse in the mountains. For purposes of comparison, that is akin to a distance greater than that from Missoula, Montana, to Chicago, Illinois.

It's interesting to note that a successful hunt, as far as Red and his staff are concerned, isn't necessarily equated with the numbers or sizes of elk taken. They view hunting as a total concept. New friends, riding a horse in the wilderness, and gaining an appreciation of how difficult an animal elk are to hunt are big parts of what he likes his hunters to experience.

Red relates two hunting tales. The first is poignant and contains a moral for us all. The second involves a gang of tough old Maine hunters whose hunt, unexpectedly, ended prematurely. Red opens the chapter by describing how a trip might be conducted.

Red Simpson

I carry out my pack trips in a little different fashion from most outfitters. We, meaning myself and my staff (guides and wranglers) read the country for our guests as we pass through it. We spend a lot of time talking about and identifying flowers, animals and their tracks, or any other living thing we might encounter. Since the Northern Rockies represent a huge geological exhibit we also discuss rock formations, how and when the Rockies were formed, and so on. I want our guests to participate, to get involved in their trips and to feel a part of the total outdoor experience.

I'm reminded of a story. I was leading a group of guests down the trail one beautiful summer morning, pointing out various things of interest. On the left I pointed out a ponderosa pine, indicating it was a good lumber species which prefers to grow on the dry south-facing mountain slopes. It so happened there were 8 people behind me and the clacking of horses' hoofs, creaking of saddle leather and other pleasant trail sounds were drowning out my voice so the last 2 or 3 people couldn't hear me. Our group, to solve the problem, would pass my words along person by person until the last one got my explanation.

Soon I came upon a strikingly-colored Indian Paintbrush. I explained it to be a flower species that grew at high elevations and the higher the altitude, the redder the flower would become. The individual behind me would pass my words on to the next person: "Here is an Indian Paintbrush," and so on. Our system worked well and everyone including myself was having a field day identifying various species of vegetation, animal tracks along the trail, and rock formations.

Finally, we arrived at a wet place in the trail which had been churned to mud by a band of elk. I was impressed by one print which was much larger than the others. I got off my horse to examine it more closely and exclaimed, "Man, what a whale of a track!" The gentleman behind me, not hearing me clearly, turned to the next rider and said, "Whale track ahead." Well, "whale track ahead" got passed down to 3 or 4 more people before someone realized there must be a mistake. I can assure you the story got jokingly passed around the campfire several times that evening to the chagrin of the originator.

Our hunting parties are limited to 6 guests and run a period of 8 days. Our hunting season runs from mid-September through early November My hunters come from all over the world, from New Zealand to France. I even have hunters from the immediate area who are tired of driving 2 hours in the dark, hunting all day and then arriving home late. They want the continuity of several days of unbroken hunting in quality country.

Our camps are unique in that we can pack the entire camp into the mountains on 4 mules. We set up 1 tent which measures 52 by 14 feet and contains 3 heating stoves. One end of the tent is enclosed for 6 guests, fully carpeted, holds 6 bunks, and has a rack over the stove to dry wet clothes.

The kitchen area is in the center of the large tent and is the hub of the camp. It contains a cookstove, eating table and cooking gear. This is where everyone congregates to prop their feet up, sip coffee and discuss the day's events. Often the air in this part of the tent is heavy with some of the wildest, tallest tales one could imagine. If that old stove could only talk! The remainder of the large tent is reserved for the guides, their gear and supplies.

With this type of arrangement, all our hunters, staff, equipment and supplies are conveniently under 1 roof. This plan solves a lot of organizational problems and makes it easier to coordinate the day's activities. Besides, it is nice and homey. I supply 1 guide per 2 hunters which has seemed to work well for us. Our fee (in 1984) is $200 per day per hunter, which comes to $1,600.00 for an 8-day hunt.

Nowadays big bulls are becoming increasingly difficult to come by, and this has put pressure on our operation. Most hunters prefer to at least harvest a reasonable representative of the species and in many instances that is a tall order to fill.

For example, the 1983 season showed a success rate for nonresident elk hunters in Montana of slightly less than 17 percent. Resident success was even lower, at about 14 percent. Another way to put it is that only 17 out of 100 nonresident elk hunters harvested an elk of any kind, bull or otherwise.

In recent seasons, we have found that many of our hunters don't measure success by reason of a kill. My personal philosophy is to foster that feeling in our hunters. Killing an elk is a great and celebrated event, making all concerned happy, but we are also sending a lot of hunters home happy who have not taken elk. I believe in a total hunting experience. We attempt to teach our hunters how a hunting camp operates as well as giving them an insight into elk as a species, and how to hunt them.

We rise every morning at 3 a.m., have breakfast, catch the horses and turn them down the trail 45 minutes or so before daylight. Before moving out, the guides and I have already conferred and picked the most likely spot to find elk, depending on weather conditions. After arriving at our hunting site, we wait until daylight and begin glassing for elk. We show our hunters how to study the terrain, examining timbered draws, patches of aspen, meadows and other "elkie" spots. If unsuccessful with binoculars, we will hike short distances and look into other hidden pockets in the hope of catching sight of the elusive critters. Generally by mid-morning, if the prospects of seeing elk are not good, we change tactics.

Sure, we could work the heavy timber during the mid-day period and find elk but we have found that our hunters require a relatively easy shot. There are several legitimate reasons for this. Most hunters are not used to the type of mountain terrain found in the Northern Rockies, and the altitude in particular seems to bother many of them. Many also have difficulty judging distances, and therefore tend to miss longer shots that naturally have a greater margin for error. We prefer to keep the shots under 200 yards and have the elk clear of heavy timber. Obviously, these self-imposed guidelines give me and my guides a handicap, but I feel this approach gives our hunters the best chance of success.

With these thoughts in mind, our party will saddle up and drop out of the high country by mid-morning. We try to locate a creek bottom or a stand of timber where there might be elk beds, tracks, or some kind of sign. Once such an area is located, we have a teaching and learning session. This part of our day generates a lot of interest and enthusiasm because many of our hunters have never seen an elk track or rub before, and it is rewarding for them. Most importantly, it shows our hunters real live evidence that there are elk in the proximity and the chance of collecting one is real.

We try to teach our hunters how to read and interpret sign, such as how to tell a bull track from a cow track or why elk trails follow certain patterns. It is personally very rewarding to me to see our hunters get excited about learning the habits of elk and how sign can unfold into a story. We often have repeat hunters, and every season their hunting and sign-reading skills improve.

We have found that after three or four days of this type of activity, some of our hunters begin to look at the animals and environment in a different way. They begin to appreciate a good mountain horse, a beautiful sunrise, or just the experience of being in the mountains during the special time of year. They enjoy an awareness they have never felt before. Believe it or not, we have had people who paid us to take them elk hunting and then left their rifles in camp, preferring to spend the day studying the environment and learning about elk. Even more unbelievable, I've even had some "hunters" come into camp without a rifle! They simply wanted to be in the mountains in the fall, breathing the frosty air. They are seeking all the life-renewing experiences to be found in a wilderness.

I recall one hunting guest who didn't bring his rifle but nevertheless enjoyed the greatest hunt he had ever experienced. He was out snow-tracking elk one day and finally managed, after considerable time, to slip in among the herd. The elk, becoming alarmed, jumped and ran but not until the hunter was literally standing in the middle of them. He was ecstatic! By the way, this man was no novice outdoorsman, having killed Kodiak bear, moose and hunted in Africa. He recalled this as his most rewarding hunt because he was able to apply the skills he had learned with us and, by himself, had been able to locate sign, sort it out, track down the elk, and very quietly slip into the herd.

The ultimate hunt for a serious hunter from back East is for us to supply the equipment, transportation and some hunting expertise. He then wants to be put into good elk habitat and left alone to try his luck. He prefers to walk a few draws or climb some ridges on his own. Of course, the ultimate culmination would be for him to fill his tag while using his own skills and instinct. However, we also have the situation in which we have to lay our jackets on the ground for a rest, place the hunter's rifle on the jacket, lay him down and point the rifle in the right direction. We do everything but squeeze the trigger. There is no question that this type of hunting experience is a much less satisfying one. We don't like to conduct our hunts in this fashion; to attempt to do so with most of our hunters would ruin their hunt.

One hunt has special meaning to me. It took place in 1972 in the Bob Marshall Wilderness. The group consisted of 2 older gentlemen from Ohio who were old hunting pals, and a father and son team from Indiana.

The father had been planning a hunt with me for several seasons, but we had never made connections. Year after year, he would call but something always intervened to spoil our arrangements. Finally, one afternoon in September he called my home and said, "Red I've got an important question to ask you. I've now got an ironclad opportunity to go hunting and my son, who was recently drafted and just completed basic training, will be home in 2 weeks. Can he and I come out and go elk hunting? I really want to spend some quality time with him before he is shipped out. I want him to get a big bull."

I just happened to have an opening and told him so. A party had cancelled a hunt and the vacancy hadn't been filled. He jumped at the opportunity and the hunt was set for the first of October.

The four men arrived at the airport on the same day, ready to enjoy a wilderness hunt. The son was a handsome, strapping kid who had the look of the Marine Corps right down to his crewcut. He cut a striking figure. His dad, a businessman in his mid-50s, was very proud of him. The other 2 hunters, a little on the heavy side and out of condition, were in their late 50s. Neither appeared to be as anxious to push elk around as were the father and son.

The next day, we drove the stock and the camp to the trailhead at the end of the road. We loaded the horses and mules with gear and people and started for camp. Everyone was on an emotional high and even our horses were in high spirits as they paced lightly down the trail. After traveling a short way, we reined in our horses and I asked my hunters to load their rifles but not to chamber a cartridge, and then place their rifles back in the saddle scabbards. This is a routine practice because on our way to camp we occasionally see bear or elk. The men all dismounted and proceeded to follow directions. One of the two older hunters took me off to the side and said, "Red, I've got a problem. I'm not sure what part of my rifle is the chamber." After some polite questioning, I realized this man knew nothing about his rifle, had never handled or fired his rifle before, and couldn't even identify the safety, which made me a little nervous.

I spent several minutes discussing the various parts of his rifle

Trail maintenance is a fact of life in the outfitting business.

and how to safely operate it. He was a little embarrassed about the situation and as I was loading him back onto his horse I had to chuckle to myself. He presented a dashing figure, sitting astride his horse. He was decked out, from head to toe, with hunter orange. I'm not sure, but I think he even wore orange long-johns.

At any rate, we again headed toward camp. About a mile out, we spied a bear foraging on the hillside. The young Marine and his dad wanted to chase after it immediately, but I held them back. "Fellas, it's getting close to dark and if we go up that ridge after that bear, we're going to get caught in the dark. We had better wait. There are, after all, 8 more days of hunting and we surely can do better." Following a few minutes of discussion, everyone agreed.

For some time, however, I had been noticing heavy dark clouds building in the west and as we rode into camp it began to snow. I knew a good storm was brewing because the mules were fidgeting and beginning to turn their backs into the wind. We quickly unloaded, fed and retired the stock for the night. Luckily, the camp was already set from a previous hunt and we were all soon sipping coffee and snuggled around a rapidly-warming stove. The tent took on a warm, homey atmosphere and everyone began to relax and gab.

But I soon got about the business of being an outfitter. I customarily examine everyone's rifle the first night in camp. And lo and behold, the gentleman who knew nothing about his rifle had, somewhere along the trail, lost a screw out of the scope mount. We checked everywhere for it, including the rifle scabbard, but it was gone. Since the scope was loose, our only choice, if we were to have a shootable rifle, was to bore sight it and use the iron sights. The young Marine took charge, since he had just finished basic training in rifle use and maintenance. After about 2 hours he had the rifle ship-shape.

With everyone now in good spirits, we settled down to our traditional first night supper, which I take great pride in preparing. The meal consisted of Norwegian meatballs with mashed potatoes and gravy, biscuits, tossed salad, and cake for dessert.

The food and warm tent did their job and soon everyone was drowsy nearly to the point of nodding off. Well, everyone started trading stories, describing where and what they had hunted. While listening, I could hear the wind whistling outside and the snow was building against the tent. I realized we were into quite a storm and I was apprehensive about the next morning's hunt. But the stories flowed late into the night, along with the consumption of large amounts of coffee, some of which was laced with a little whiskey.

It proved to be an interesting evening. All of us learned a little about each other and generally enjoyed the camaraderie, but I disrupted the comfortable atmosphere at midnight and announced that it was bed-time; 3 a.m. would arrive quickly. There were elk to be hunted the next day!

My alarm went off way too early, or at least I thought so. Stumbling toward the kitchen, I found a lantern to light, dressed and stepped out to check the weather. A clear sky full of thousands of shimmering stars greeted me. The storm had passed over, leaving behind 6 inches of powdery, fresh snow. "It's going to be one of those perfect days to hunt. A snowstorm followed by clear weather, plus new tracking snow. The elk should be moving and feeding," I thought.

Stepping back inside I rustled up hotcakes, bacon, eggs and coffee. The aroma soon had folks moving toward the kitchen. The wranglers, in the meantime, dressed and disappeared into the darkness to locate and saddle the horses. Shortly, hunters and guides convened in the kitchen to stoke their bellies full of grub. Everyone had a good appetite and ate plenty. Guides in particular are noted for having bottomless pits for stomachs, but mine couldn't touch the young soldier. Here was a guy who liked to eat, but after hiding three or four plates of hotcakes even he was holding his stomach. He was that kid of kid, sociable and friendly, the type of guy a person could warm up to real easy. He even helped me with the breakfast dishes and I enjoyed his company.

Following a few last minute preparations, we saddled up in the darkness and rode off down the trail. Although it wouldn't be daylight for another 45 minutes, the woods were clearly illuminated by starlight reflecting off the snow. The trail led up a mountain, switching back and forth several times, until it broke out into a small meadow. We stopped here and I had everyone check his rifle before we got close to where I suspected the elk to be. We continued on for another 15 minutes and entered a small grove of trees where we tied the horses, loosened the cinches and checked our gear one more time.

We walked toward a large alpine park where I'd often seen elk before and after a few minutes cut several fresh elk tracks leading into the meadow. All 7 of us — 4 hunters, 2 guides and myself — started easing along the fringes of the meadow, just inside the timber. Soon I was able to see in the dim pre-dawn light the outlines of elk, about 30 head, feeding in the meadow. I glassed the herd and determined there was 1 good 6-point, 1 4- or 5-point, and 2 spike bulls in the group. The herd was totally unaware of our presence.

I asked a guide to drop back into the timber and take the father and son around to the west side of the meadow and loop behind the elk. "We will give you about 10 minutes and then we will try for a shot," I said. "When we shoot, look for the elk to break out in your direction."

The allotted time passed and I moved the 2 older hunters a short distance through the trees to position them for a better shot. I wanted not only to get them within 200 yards or less of the elk, but also to find a tree or stump on which they could rest their rifles. We all tried to keep our hands and feet warm as we sat in the snow a few more minutes, waiting for better shooting light. In the meantime, the bigger bull had drifted to the west toward the other hunters.

Everything seemed to be about as right as it could possibly be, so I asked the guide to get one of the gentlemen in position to shoot. I then helped the other hunter get ready by resting his repaired, scopeless rifle on a stump. About that time the first hunter shot at 1 of the spikes. My hunter became very excited upon hearing his pal's shot and proceeded to unload his rifle at an elk. His shots didn't come close because he was completely unfamiliar with using iron sights and because he was very nervous. Meanwhile, the other hunter, after 4 or 5 more shots, had managed to knock the spike down. We had at least 1 elk for sure.

The elk herd, momentarily confused by all the shooting, milled around in the meadow and allowed my hunter time to reload his rifle. He sent another barrage at the elk and, to his delight, killed a cow. So now we had 2 elk down. My mind flashed to the big bull and I realized I had lost track of it. I thought he might have drifted toward the other hunters, but I hadn't heard a shot. Our 2 successful hunters were very happy, jumping around and patting each other on the back. They couldn't believe what had happened — their elk hunting trip had just started and it was a success.

As we were butchering their elk, the guide and other 2 hunters came back and reported they had not seen the big bull. He had given them the slip, so we completed the butchering chores,took the 2 successful hunters — who by now were "plumb wore out" — back to camp. All they wanted to do was get to camp, where they didn't want anything else but some whiskey-flavored coffee and some sleep.

The turn of events had really gotten the father and son aroused, especially the son. He wanted an elk in the worst way. The father was indifferent about killing an elk himself, but wanted to be with his son when and if he got an elk. The 2 were close and wanted to share the experience. Once we'd deposited the 2 older hunters in camp, a guide and I loaded up the father and son and headed up the trail into another area. We intended to work a large timbered basin in which I'd taken elk before.

It was conspicuously quiet and we didn't cut a single elk track as we rode the horses nearly to the head of the basin. Even though the rut was waning and it was 3 o'clock in the afternoon, I decided to try bugling. We dismounted and I blew a bugle toward the timber across the basin. Fifteen minutes of waiting produced no results and I bugled again, not really expecting to rouse a bull. We waited 15 more minutes and I started to put my bugle back into my daypack when way, way off we heard a barely-audible, high-pitched whine. The son heard the answer too, and it was like throwing a switch. He was hot to take after the bull. "Let's give it a try," I agreed. "We will work into the head of the basin where the trees thin out and see if we can catch the bull in an opening."

We rode high into the basin, tied the horses and hiked up into the thinning timber. I settled in and bugled again and got a quick response. The bull was very close! We continued moving until we worked our way to within 400 yards of the bull. He was out of sight, below us in the timber on the floor of the basin. I put the hunters out in front of me and bugled again, getting the quick answer, but the bull had begun to move away from us at an angle. Somehow I had to turn the bull back, so I tried 1 more trick.

I repositioned the hunters behind some cover providing a view into a small meadow and, bugling as I went, I ran in the opposite direction in a direct line for about 300 yards. My idea was to convince the bull that his challenger was moving away. He returned a bugle, and the sound indicated that he had stopped. So far so good. Moving away again, I bugled a second time. He answered and was moving back toward my hunters. To increase the bull's interest, I banged and scraped a dead limb on a tree to imitate a bull raking a tree with his antlers.

The bull then began to circle downwind and I knew it wouldn't be long before he scented the hunters. This time, moving toward the bull, I bugled and pushed him back upwind. The bull played this cat-and-mouse game with me for 20 minutes with the hunters in the middle. As I was moving from place to place, I would catch and occasional glimpse of the 19-year-old Marine and I could see that he and his dad were getting very tense over this whole process.

Finally, the bull stepped into the meadow and swung his head back and forth as he tried to locate the source of the bugling. He was very edgy and I knew the son would have to shoot quickly. Then his rifle roared and I saw the bull wince, lunge forward a few yards and stumble into a pile. The Marine had his elk, a beautiful 6-point. Congratulations and handshakes were shared by hunters and guides alike — the tension was over, ending in success.

The guide and I field dressed and caped the elk. The father, who was very pleased to have shared the experience with his son, encouraged him to have the trophy mounted as a memento of their first elk hunt together. He readily agreed.

At camp we had one heck of a celebration, with toasts aplenty, with 2 bulls and a cow taken on the first day of the hunt. Our meat pole was sagging. The rest of the hunt, however, was uneventful as the we spent 6 more days in the field without seeing another elk. The father didn't care, though, as he was quite contented about the entire situation.

About 8 weeks later, the hunting season over, I was out in the barn storing hunting equipment and pulling horseshoes when my wife handed me a letter. It was from the young Marine's father. It read: "Red, I want to thank you for the greatest hunt I've ever experienced in my entire life. It was an unforgettable experience that I shared with my son. I want to tell you also, 3 days after we arrived home from Montana, my son was shipped to Vietnam. Eight hours after arriving in Saigon, he was killed in a helicopter crash."

Six years went by without again hearing from the man when another letter came. "If you're ever back East, please stop at our home and see us," he wrote. Fate often intervenes in strange ways because shortly after receiving that letter my wife and I had reason to visit Ohio. On our way through Indiana, we stopped and called. The father was very happy to hear we were in town and insisted we come to their home for dinner. We readily accepted the invitation.

He had a very nice home with a large fireplace in the living room. Over the fireplace hung the mount of the bull his son had taken on our hunt. On one side of the bull was a picture of the father, his son, the horses they rode on the hunt, and myself kneeling in front with my elk bugle in hand. On the other side of the bull was a picture of his son dressed in his Marine uniform taken just before he was shipped over to Vietnam. The father told me he had just recently put the elk over the fireplace because he and his wife had finally been able to accept the death of their son. It was a very touching moment in my life. It made all the bad trails, poor hunts and other assorted hardships associated with the outfitting business worthwhile.

A month or so after I got back home, I was rummaging through old boxes full of equipment and found the elk bugle I had used to call in the young Marine's trophy. I packaged it and sent it to the father, and it now hangs over the fireplace with the other mementoes.

But let me finish our story-telling on a happy note. I want to tell you about 4 hunters who came to my camp from Maine. It is one of those hunts that happens maybe 1 or 2 times in a lifetime. It occurred in November 1966.

Six hunting buddies from Maine contracted my outfit to take them elk hunting. I guess all hunters from Maine have 2 things in common. When I picked them up at the airport, they all had on L.L. Bean boots and all were dressed in red wool from top to bottom. They literally got off the plane ready to go hunting.

At the baggage area we collected their gear, which consisted of one big square knapsack each. I figured they would have a ton of gear, but one knapsack per man was it. Then I glanced at their rifles and saw they all had iron-sighted .30-.30s. Oh boy! "They brought their deer rifles. I'll never get these guys an elk," I thought to myself. We were going to be in for an interesting hunt, if nothing else, especially since 5 of the 6 were in their 60s and the sixth was 72 years old.

But the guys turned out to be an easy-going group. When we arrived at the trailhead leading into the Bitterroot Mountains, I started to explain how to drive a horse. "These are the reins and

A trophy bull elk stands in a mountain meadow, his antlers glistening in the light of early morning.

we steer a horse this way," I said. They replied: "Aw, we'll figure that out. Just get us into elk country."

The ride into camp was uneventful except for the heavy snowfall which was still coming down when we slipped into camp. The down jacket the experienced outfitter from Montana wore was soaked and clinging to his body — my body — like a wet rag. I was shivering and shaking, in bad need of dry clothes and a cup of coffee, but the boys from Maine, dressed in their wool, were toasty warm and thoroughly enjoying their trip.

That evening we learned how the men hunted deer in Maine. They used canoes a lot, paddling up and down streams to various hunting camps they had set up. They would float-hunt or tromp the woods and had enjoyed many fruitful hunts. Eventually I discreetly worked the conversation around to firearms. I asked them plenty of questions about how well they could handle and shoot their rifles. I told them elk are very large animals, some as big as a horse, and are usually shot at long distances. "Elk are most often hunted with a .30-.06, .270 or sometimes a 7mm," I said. I really made an effort to tell them I was concerned about their choice of rifles. Finally, the older of the 6 looked at me and said, "Red, you just get us within what you consider good range and we will take care of the rest."

We left camp the next morning well before daylight and I still wasn't sure what I was going to do with my 6 .30-.30-toting hunters. Two hours later we tied the horses in a stand of trees just as it began to snow big, moist flakes. In a few minutes it was snowing so hard I didn't think we would even be able to see the elk if we did get near them. On the bright side, at least my hunters wouldn't have to worry about the snow blotting out the lenses of a scope.

As we prepared to begin our hunt, I quietly told each of the guides: "This effort was just going to be a walk in the snow. Let's spread out and see what happens, but don't expect too much."

We had no sooner walked around the first sidehill and there, to my surprise, across a small draw we spied a herd of elk feeding about 200 yards away. Knowing we would have to get closer to offer our hunters any real chance at a shot, we started down into the brushy draw. We commenced to make one heck of a racket as all 6 hunters and the guides were slipping and sliding down the snow-slickened slope. We hadn't gone very far when the oldest hunter tapped me on the shoulder and said, "Hey Red, take us back to where we were and let us take a shot." I replied: "Hell, you can't hit an elk at that distance in this storm with an open-sighted .30-.30. We can hardly see them." Well, he convinced me to go back and let him try a shot anyway, I figured the elk would be gone by the time we climbed out of the draw, with all the slipping, falling and scratching around we were doing.

After retracing our steps, we found the elk were still where we'd first seen them. I tried to look them over with my binoculars but in the mass of heavy white snowflakes all I could make out were the brown shapes of the animals. I couldn't tell bulls from cows. The old gentleman had grown impatient from all the delaying, however, and said, "Red, why don't you just step back a little and let me shoot." I did and he promptly raised his rifle and shot off-hand, dropping what later proved to be a cow.

The heavily-falling snow and thick brush muffled the sound of the shot and the entire band became confused, dropped into the draw and started right for us. The rest of the hunters were, I had to admit, cool. They calmly jacked shells into the chambers of their rifles and got into position to shoot. One man even took off his hat.

It didn't take the elk long to cover the 200 yards and we could soon hear the brush popping and crashing as the elk cleared the draw. This promptly became the shortest guided hunt I'd ever conducted. In the next few minutes, everyone filled his tag — even one of my guides. Fifteen minutes after daylight of the first day of hunting, every hunter on the trip had an elk. It was the most incredible sight I'd ever seen. Elk were laying everywhere, including 1 nice 5-point bull and a 6-point with only 1 antler. Examination of the 1-antlered bull showed the pedicel on the antlerless side had been damaged, causing the antler not to grow.

My Maine hunters were jumping up and down, exclaiming, "Montana is the greatest place in the world to hunt." How could I argue? It obviously was! We had one slight problem, however. The hunters had paid for an 8-day trip, but it was successfully completed with 7 days 23 hours and 45 minutes left in the hunt.

We just changed our method of operation. Some of the guys slept late, played cards, or hiked in the mountains around camp. A few took long day rides with the horses, learning horsemanship and studying the country,. Of course, we all ate like kings, preparing more than one gourmet meal. After about 5 days, the old boys were like veteran mountain men, better than some guides I've had. I really had to hand it to the men from Maine. Ninety-five percent of the hunters I've ever guided would never have gone out that first morning because of the foul weather. Being dedicated hunters from a part of the country that also has rough winters, they thought nothing of a little snow.

Robert L. Stoney Burk

"If I had to sum up successful elk hunting in 3 words, they are: persistence, persistence, persistence. Impatience is the worst enemy of the elk hunter while persistence is his best friend. I've never seen anyone kill an elk while sitting in front of a television set, or off a bar stool. If you're going to talk to me about elk hunting, you had best get out and hunt. Persistence is the key to success." — Stoney Burk

Touched by a Bull

Stoney Burk, a 42-year-old native Montanan, currently lives in a small town tucked up against the East Face of the Rocky Mountains. He came from an outdoor-oriented family and killed his first mule deer buck at 12 years of age. Stoney helped his father harvest an elk 2 years later and bagged himself a nice 5-point bull at age 16. These early experiences hooked him and he has become a very dedicated hunter and outdoorsman. For most of his career, he rifle hunted but since the mid-1970s has become a serious bowhunter as well — taking a tremendous bull in 1976.

Stoney describes a series of events occurring in 1976 and 1978 that helped him gain enough experience and self confidence to handle a very unusual situation that occurred during an elk hunt in 1983. His story begins with the 1976 hunt and we gratefully acknowledge permission from *American Hunter* magazine to use the first portion of this chapter as the story of that 1976 hunt was told in that publication's July 1978 issue.

Stoney Burk

I have enjoyed archery since age 8, but archery was a hobby and not a serious endeavor. For many years, I had used archery season as an excuse to get out and scout the high country but never gave it a serious effort. I would not allow myself to settle for a medium-sized buck when I knew I could get a big one in rifle season. So, the years passed as enjoyable years but with little big game success as an archer. I always took a few grouse and rabbits, but not big game.

Sometime in early 1975 I decided to be serious. Before the 1975 archery season I purchased a compound bow, a dozen aluminum target arrows and traded in my take-down bow. After a short period of practice with my new compound, the arrows were grouping well enough for me to be confident in the field. But, there was one big problem. I had already made commitments to some friends for the regular rifle season. Because I had promised to hunt with them, I had to wait until the 1976 season to really try for elk with the bow. I didn't give my heart to the archery hunt that fall.

I believe that attitude makes the difference in hunting. Many hunters say that you must have a $500 rifle with a 9-power scope to score consistently, or the best compound bow, etc. For 14 years as a rifle hunter, I used a plain model 721 Remington .270 and had every bit as much success with both elk and deer as my more expensively equipped friends. It does no good to have the very best of equipment unless you are physically and mentally ready to hunt.

I was a fighter pilot in the Air Force for 8 years. It didn't matter how fancy your calculations were — the name of the game is to put the bomb on the target. The same theory applies in hunting. You have to put yourself in a position to make the shot and to be ready for it under the very worst circumstances. If you have decent equipment, your attitude will make the difference.

The 1976 season was different from seasons of past years. Planning for this hunt began right after the last day of the 1975 season. Then, as soon as spring weather permitted, I started practicing with my bow. By mid-summer I had mounted a sight on the bow to aid in judging azimuth and elevation.

It is critical, I believe, for archery hunters to practice in real life settings as it is for them to practice on a controlled range. I placed bales of hay out in the woods and practiced difficult shots from various angles. Many of the deer and elk I've bagged with a rifle have been in heavy cover, often with only a small patch open for a kill shot. I tried to simulate these conditions and this practice proved invaluable.

I've found few people willing to pay the price in physical output needed to bring consistent success in elk hunting. Rain, snow, freezing cold, choking thirst, and hunger are often a regular part of the hunt, and I'll gladly endure them all to get my elk.

I traveled about 2 miles along a mountaintop before finally locating a big bull down in a heavily timbered basin. The bull had an ivory-tipped rack of at least 6 points. I stalked the bull until coming to within 40 yards of him in the heavy brush. He was facing me, so I couldn't try for a shot. I will not shoot a head-on shot with a bow, because I feel it is a gross injustice for any hunter to take a poor shot at these beautiful creatures. I wanted a clean kill or none at all. I waited tensely for him to turn broadside.

The bull finally caught my scent and started to walk nervously away in dense lodgepole and underbrush. He stopped at about 40 yards and turned broadside, but only a small area about a foot wide was open between 2 trees. I was so excited that my bow was shaking as I drew the arrow to the hilt. The sight settled on the rib cage just behind the shoulder. I stabilized and let fly! The arrow was going true to the point but was off in azimuth just enough to graze one of the trees and it ricochetted in front of the animal.

My heart sunk as he bolted, but I was thankful that it was a clean miss. I spent all the next day trying to locate him and after about 12 miles of climbing, slipping, lurching and hunting, I gave up for another week. One inch in azimuth had made the difference between success or failure with this particular bull.

All that next week my thoughts were on the bull that got away. It had taken me 3 days to locate him, and I had blown it.

Elk bugle during mating season roughly from mid-September to early October, but they vary from year to year depending on weather, pressure and location. I've heard and seen elk bugling in the Mogollon Rim country of Arizona in the first week of September and I've heard them as late as October 15 in Montana. I knew I had to hunt hard the next week or face the possibility of missing another chance in this season. I had made up my mind not to settle for anything smaller than a 5-point bull, because I was confident that I could locate one that big during the regular season.

By Wednesday, September 22, the fever got me again. I packed my packsack, sleeping bag, and enough food to last for 2 days. Daylight found me a mile back from the road. I hiked, glassed and bugled several basins, traveling about 3 miles by 11 a.m. Finally I got a response — a short, gutteral grunt followed by the battle call of a big bull.

I clambered down the mountain, over windfalls and chest-high brush to get to where he was. After an hour, I finally had closed to within 100 yards and caught a glimpse of thrashing horns. The bull was ravaging a small spruce tree with tosses of his heavy rack. Then disaster. At 50 yards he caught my scent and nervously strutted off, too proud to bolt and too wary to stay.

I chased that bull until I was sure my tongue was touching my shoelaces. Once I was within 25 yards of him and could count 7 points on each side of his oddly-shaped rack, but could not get a good shot because of brush and heavy timber. By nightfall I was nearly dead from exhaustion and thirst. It had been a truly exhilarating day.

The sleeping bag was heaven that night. I figured the bull had taken me well over 5 miles up and down the timber-strewn mountain before I finally gave up at dusk. There is no failure in hunting as far as I'm concerned; I had spent one of the most beautiful days of my life that day, 20 miles from the nearest house, alone, chasing a magnificent bull elk through beautiful country. If that is failure, what is success?

At daylight the next morning I was within a mile of where I'd last seen the wary bull. I tried several times with the bugle but got no response. Then I traveled about 3 more miles along the mountain crest, bugling and scanning the basins. Finally about 10:30 I heard an instant bellowing response from a spruce-covered basin. While searching hard to locate the bull, much to my surprise a magnificent elk stepped into a small clearing about 1,000 yards below me. The morning sun glinted off his massive rack as he swung his head in my direction. I ducked behind cover and tried to figure out a way to get off the steep mountain rim down into the basin without spooking him.

About a quarter-mile to the north was a step, heavily timbered slope. I worked my work along the ridge, using the terrain to cover my movement, and then dropped over the steep incline. The noise seemed unbearable in the dry underbrush. Elk have a tremendously acute sense of smell and hearing. If he heard me or caught my scent, he would be gone.

I estimated the bull would be somewhere within 500 yards when I reached the basin floor. I moved cautiously along a feeder ridge trying to see through the dense cover. Suddenly, a twig snapped! A flash of antlers drew my focus to about 70 yards to my right front. The bull had apparently decided to come up the way I was coming down. He swung away and crashed out of sight as he ran perpendicular to the left of my path. I grabbed my bugle in a furtive attempt to confuse him and let out a loud squeal. The crashing stopped! I wondered if he had gone out of hearing or had actually responded.

Years of experience in similar situations told me to calm myself and be cautious. I must have moved 20 yards before I could see over the break of the hill. Nothing.

Then, off to my left, movement! Antlers! The tips of the big rack were swinging back and forth like a radar antenna. I ducked and made about 4 nerve-wrenching steps forward and then cautiously raised up.

The bull was standing broadside in chest-high huckleberry

"It ain't all fun." Stoney Burk with a quarter of his elk on his back.

brush about 40 yards from me, the maximum distance I want to shoot at an elk with a bow. I judged the elevation and let go. The huge animal was just starting to move with the arrow struck. A loud "oomph" came from the bull, followed by crashing brush. I frantically searched for the shaft sticking from his side, but could not see it. Did I miss? The bull lunged out of sight.

All of a sudden, I heard a thunderous crash. The sound was unmistakable; one I've heard so many times before. I ran toward the sound, only half believing and yet knowing the elk was dead.

There he lay — a good 6-point bull.

I quickly put 3 more arrows into the animal, while trying to suppress the instinctive victory cries rising in my throat. I've seen many elk that were down get up and sometimes run hundreds of yards. I took no chances, but the extra arrows were not needed. I later found that the first arrow had pierced the animal's heart and continued on into the opposite shoulder.

My excitement was too much to contain. I let out a loud war whoop and did a little victory jig. I took numerous pictures with my 35mm camera, being glad that I always pack a camera to catch this kind of unforgettable moment.

The next two days were spent back on earth. My father, Ted, and my brothers, Dale and Arlie, helped me to get the bull out, but not without plenty of trouble and work. We borrowed a horse, but the horse slipped off the trail on 2 occasions with 2 quarters of the elk. My dad was stepped on, kicked, and the horse completely rolled over him once; so we finally left the front quarters and brought the horse out empty. Dale and I backpacked out about 175 pounds each. I went back the next day with my brother Arlie's boy, Stan, and backpacked out the neck and front quarters. It took me another full day to clean, cut and wrap the meat. Was it worth it? You bet!

Another great elk hunting experience, occurred in late September 1978 when Silas Torrey, my hunting partner of many years, and I planned a bowhunting trip in northwest Montana. The country there is densely clothed with vegetation and has numerous wet, boggy areas. The undergrowth is mostly alder, snow and huckleberry bushes. The overstory consists of evergreens, western larch, Douglas fir and spruce. The mountains, cross-hatched with ridgelines demarcating drainages, rise to elevations of 5,500 to 7,500 feet. It is the type of country that offers cover, forage and isolation for a sizable elk population; however, because of the nature of the country, it can be difficult to see an elk even as close as 40 yards.

We would get up well before dawn, leave the truck and hike several miles up on the high ridges and at the first light bugle the basins. One afternoon, after a slow morning, I bugled down into a timbered basin and a bull answered. After exchanging several grunts and bugles, the bull was cooking pretty good and I could sense he was working himself into a frenzy. He showed no inclination to move, however, so I worked myself down through the timber to within about 200 yards of him. After a few minutes I could tell by the volume of his bugling that he was beginning to come my way, so I searched the brush for a good ambush site. I positioned at the edge of a small, damp brush-filled meadow with a huge spruce tree to my left. It was a super place to set up and try to grunt the bull in. In front of the spruce was a barrier of waist-high huckleberry bushes with sprouts running up chest high.

As I settled next to the big tree and behind the screening brush, I noticed a well-used game trail running beside the base of the spruce. It appeared to be a natural travel route for the bull. I expected him to cut the trail while coming to me and that thought gave me an added degree of confidence.

No sooner had I settled in than he bellowed an excited, crackling bugle across the meadow. It was a fantastic moment. He came into the clearing, head laid back, eyes red, and bugling as he walked. I could almost feel his breath on my face. No slip-ups! Stay cool! Upon seeing his big, ivory-tipped rack bobbing through the clearing, I squatted lower in the brush and cramped myself against the tree. I can remember thinking to myself: "He is coming right to me."

He was smoking hot and looking for trouble. Neck stretched out and still bugling, his heavy 6-point rack was rotating from side to side as he searched the timber for his foe. He then cut the trail, laid his antlers back along his flanks and broke into a fast walk — coming right at me. I'm sure he didn't see me.

My plan was to let him walk past me and quarter an arrow into the back of his ribs, but it didn't work out that way. He evidently had my bugling pinpointed and that was exactly where he was going. I was, in effect, trapped. Thinking the bull would pass, I hadn't gotten my bow into a position to shoot but had to remain crouched. Ultimately, I could have reached out with an arrow and touched his nose. But I couldn't move.

I had never before been so close to a live elk. In his frame of mind, I didn't really know what he would do as he had closed the distance between us to 2 yards and stopped. I had to make a move or he'd walk right over me. Slowly, I started to stand, adjusting my bow while rising. The bull immediately threw his head back and jumped sideways, putting his butt to me like a spooked horse might, and trotted off. It all happened so fast I didn't get off a shot.

I learned a costly lesson that day. By very slowly rising to a shooting posture, I thought the bull might stop long enough to offer a shot; but, despite being so close, I should have given the bull a chance to turn and walk by. I had only a few seconds to make a critical decision and it turned out to be the wrong one. Looking back on that incident, I realize I really had no chance. The bull's reflexes were too fast.

Now, keep that incident in mind and I'll tell you about my experience regarding something similar that happened on a 1983 hunt. Silas and I planned a 14-day combination Bighorn sheep and elk hunt in the Absaroka Mountains north of Yellowstone Park. The country there is remote and difficult to hunt, but contains a sizable elk population including some excellent bulls. We placed ourselves at an additional disadvantage because we were bowhunting.

We packed in several miles and set up camp. We hunted hard for 9 days and saw plenty of elk, but even though it was the week of September 16th, we couldn't get the big bulls fired up. I saw 7 different bulls in one 15-minute period and later passed several close shots at a spike and cows. Silas had similar experiences but we never really got into the good rut. So, Silas and I decided to change areas, moving 200 miles into a totally different range of mountains.

I looked up and there was a nice 5-point bull peeking down the ridge.

That country is made up of high alpine basins combining to make huge drainage systems. The cover, in the creek bottoms and on the north slopes, is predominantly dense, wet stands of lodgepole and spruce. The south slopes are lined vertically with rock-studded avalanche chutes full of alpine vegetation and clumps of beargrass and timber. Light stands of Douglas fir, spruce and lodgepole were the primary cover.

We packed in 8 miles with the horses and set camp on a bench near a small lake. Our plan was to ride the horses out of camp before daylight, picket them, and bugle the basins while hunting on foot. About noon we would ride back to camp, catch a couple of hours sleep, and then make an evening hunt.

It was now September 27 and Silas and I were concerned about the waning rut. We hadn't been able to get the big bulls cranking in the Absarokas and had wasted 3 days changing locations.

The first morning we worked ourselves along the crest of a high alpine ridge. On our left the ridge broke off steeply and fell into a heavily timbered basin. In the grey pre-dawn light, we stopped on the ridge overlooking a steep clearing and I let out a bugle followed by a chortle. Eee-Oh-h-h-h-e-e-E-E-E---E-E-e-e-uk!-uk!-uk! A bull immediately answered and he was close. He followed with two more bellows and Silas said, "He's coming! He's coming!" We quickly dropped off the crest of the ridge and ran so as to position ourselves better so we could intercept the bull. I located in a fringe of timber with most of the meadow above me.

Without speaking, Silas moved off about 50 yards to position himself between me and the bull. Even though Silas was out of view, I knew about where he was and would try to bring the bull past him. The set-up was perfect: we were positioned well and the bull was bugling every few minutes. He sounded mad and I had a good feeling that we would nail him.

I buried myself between several clumps of beargrass and grunted. To my surprise a second bull, in the trees above the first, bugled. For about 5 minutes the bulls and I bugled and grunted back and forth and neither bull showed any inclination to move. By now I was excited. I knew it was just a matter of time until 1 of the bulls or Silas made a move. I had a vivid mental picture of Silas creeping through the timber, zeroing in on 1 of the bulls.

Another 15 minutes went by and the 2 bulls were still cranking, but not moving. I figured fine, I'll just keep talking to them so Silas can move in. All of a sudden I heard a grunt come from the crest of the meadow directly above me. I looked up and saw a 5-point bull peeking over the top. By now, I was really going crazy. Three grunting, bugling bulls were within 150 yards of me.

The 5-point proceeded down the grassy slope toward me. Situated above halfway between the bull and me was a single, stubby alpine spruce which the bull began to demolish. He worked the tree for a minute or 2 and then grunted. This caused the other 2 bulls to bugle. He stared in their direction for a few minutes and then lowered his head and continued raking. I bugled, trying to make things happen but it was apparent that all 3 bulls were staying put.

I thought Silas was working toward the 2 bulls in the timber, so I decided to stalk the 5-point. About 20 yards below and in line with the bull was a thick, brushy spruce about 20 feet tall. By keeping the tree between us, I might be able to get close enough to the 5-point bull to get a shot. Besides, if I spooked the 5-point, Silas would still have a chance at one of the other 2 bulls.

My mind buzzed over similar situations where changing positions had blown the hunt, while on the other hand making a move sometimes caused favorable things to happen. I silently wished Silas luck with the other 2 bulls and, with some reluctance, I left my prime position.

Crouching low, I eased my way along the side of the hill and fell in behind the bushy spruce. I loved being there, in that place, at that point in my life. The pre-dawn was crisp and the air was calm. The tops of my boots were wet from the cold dew and in a few minutes, if all went well, I was going to take one of the most sought-after big game species in the world.

I took a few slow, stooped steps toward the spruce tree and suddenly one of the original 2 bulls stepped into the meadow about 150 yards from the 5-point. Murphy's law had struck.

The bull was a dandy, his long ivory-tipped tines accentuated by his heavy dark-brown, almost-black, antlers. He looked toward the 5-point, laid his rack back and cut loose with a series of deep grunts and coughs. His side heaved in and out with each grunt. Steam rolled out of his mouth as if coming out of a boiler.

Placing my bow with the nocked arrow under me, I quickly sank on my belly into the clumps of beargrass which were tall enough to conceal me. The only thing showing was the tip of my camouflage stocking hat.

I grunted and the big bull walked directly toward me, closing the distance between us to 150 yards. It appeared as though he would come right in. I felt confident about getting a shot. Then, while I laid there trembling with excitement, the worst possible thing happened. The 5-point decided to walk down the slope, by the spruce tree, right for me. I assumed that since he was a young bull, he probably was more curious about my grunting than anything else. But I couldn't believe that he had picked this critical moment, just as the big bull was coming, to make his move.

I thought, "OK, if this bull comes into point-blank range, I'll take him." I thought about the old "bird-in-hand" theory. In addition, we only had 2 days left to hunt.

Then my thoughts flashed back to the lesson of that 1978 hunt. Let the bull come. Let him veer off, don't try to take him prematurely. I had my plan and was going to stick with it.

I was laying on my belly, facing uphill with my arms tucked under me and my neck stretched so tight my eyes blurred. I watched the bull plod down the slope oblivious to my presence. He was so close his breathing sounded like air being forced out of a bellows. My eyeballs were stretched so tight I felt like I was looking through the top of my skull.

Easy, I coached myself. Let him pass. Slip it in behind the ribs when he's looking away. My legs felt like chunks of dead wood and my neck was cramping badly.

Logically, the bull should turn. The incline was very steep. The sensible and easier way would be for him to turn and go sidehill. I told myself again: "Wait! Wait! Stick to your plan."

Unbelievably, the bull didn't turn and was nearly on top of me. I lowered my head very slightly, almost touching my chin to the ground. Otherwise, I was stone still.

The bull took a few more steps and his hoofs, incredibly, came into my line of vision. I couldn't believe what was happening! The bull was going to walk right up my back! Of course, in the position I had been trapped in, I had no hope of getting a shot. If I'd had a spear, yes, but not with a bow. The bull took another step and I could almost feel the grass move. Out of the corner of my eye, I could see his sides heaving in and out as he breathed, mere inches from my shoulder. I could hear his nose working, inhaling and exhaling with soft whooshing sounds as he tried to solve the riddle.

Suddenly I felt a light tap on my shoulder, which I assume was his nose, followed by a great blast of exhaled air. Then the bull bolted! A loud grunt that actually sounded like a "woof."

I jumped up immediately, but my numbed legs refused to cooperate and I nearly fell. Steadying myself, I saw the bull looking at me while he trotted broadside about 30 yards away in an arc up the steep slope. I drew back, anchored and let the arrow go. It passed under his chest, missing him cleanly. Amazingly, after all that had happened, the bull stopped behind the spruce tree and bugled. The big bull, which I had lost track of, was still standing where I'd last seen him and he answered with a responding bugle!

I quickly laid back down, thinking crazy thoughts. Maybe the big bull wanted to see what had alarmed the 5-point and would give me a second opportunity. Down he came to the spruce tree, where he cut the original line of travel the 5-point had taken. The big bull stopped and smelled the ground. Again, I was caught belly down in the big clearing. He now was only 20 yards away and all I needed him to do was look away at the 5-point and I could raise and shoot. But no such luck!

Suddenly, his ears came forward and he became nervous. The rising sun had heated the wind currents and they had given me away. My tell-tale scent had been carried to the elk's nostrils.

I thought, "NOW, quick, before he explodes." I stood up hoping for a split second of hesitation on the bull's part, but it wasn't to be. A few giant lunges and he was out of range. Another smaller bull then came into the clearing before the drama was over, but things didn't work out for a shot. Silas and I regrouped and discussed the morning's events. We were both emotionally drained, but excited about having had such a once-in-a-lifetime experience. After all, a morning like that is what makes bowhunting so enjoyable and rewarding.

In all candor, I've hesitated to tell this story but is the absolute truth. Recently I had an opportunity to discuss this hunt with Larry Jones, a well-known and experienced elk hunter. He wasn't surprised at all and went on to tell me he had taken a bull at somewhere around 12 feet. Silas took a bull at 17 feet and his brother almost took one at about the same distance. So, while it takes a special set of circumstances to get a bull within a few feet of you, it obviously can be done. I've bugled quite a few bulls in and I know others have had close encounters. I wouldn't hesitate one minute about taking a truth serum or lie detector test to verify this story. It happened and this type of experience makes me absolutely love elk hunting. I ended up bagging a nice 4-point bull with my rifle in 1983, but I'll never forget that tremendous experience when I was touched by a bull.

· ·

Question: Stoney, you have been very successful bugling and grunting elk. Would you describe your technique?

Burk: I like to walk the high, main ridgelines and drop off either side into the different basins and bugle. Some areas, like northwest Montana, are ideal for this type of hunting. Many of these main ridgelines have diverging finger ridges that offer access to even bigger sections of country. A lot of basins can be covered with a minimum of time and effort.

Some say not to bugle more than once every 20 minutes. I don't believe that. I may bugle as frequently as every 2 or 3 minutes or as infrequently as every 30 minutes, depending on how far the lay of the land permits the sound to carry. Heavy timber will muffle the sound while an entire basin may be bugled from a high ridge. In other words, I won't bugle again until walking the distance which puts me out of hearing range.

Let's say I worked down off a ridge into a drainage that I want to bugle. After bugling once and waiting 10 minutes, I'll bugle again. If nothing stirs, I'll bugle with a grunt or chortle at the end. Many times I've given up on a basin but would try a bugle with a chortle or a chortle alone and finally raise a bull. When the chortle is done alone, the first sound is drawn out. E-E-E-E-euk-euk-euk. I don't know why, but a lot of bulls won't respond until the chortle is used.

Question: You said there is one shot on an elk that you won't take with a bow. Would you elaborate?

Burk: The kill area presented with a head-on view is very small and is surrounded by heavy muscle and bones of the shoulder and the thick cartilage of the brisket. Unless the jugular is cut or an arrow is slid into the chest cavity through the small opening between the ribs at the base of the neck vertebrae, the elk will be non-fatally wounded. I always prefer shooting broadside or slightly quartering away. Stick the arrow or bullet right behind the shoulder.

Question: You talk about persistence as being the key to successful elk hunting. What do you mean?

Burk: I can best answer your question by telling you about my friend Silas Torrey. He is a dedicated elk hunter. He is an endurance man in prime physical condition. He thinks nothing of going into the mountains for days, alone, hunting for elk. He is a guy who gets out and gets it done. I'm confident he has seen and passed up more elk than 90 percent of the elk hunters in the field. In summary, Silas is a man who is willing to pay the price and to suffer the hardships involved in taking elk. You need that attitude for success.

Let me diverge here and interject some of my personal philosophy. Killing an elk doesn't necessarily make a successful hunt. Success is putting myself in a position to take an elk. I love to hunt and harvest elk, but I'm fulfilled just hiking in elk country. It's the total experience that counts. However, when one pursues a venture with the diligence that pure enjoyment brings, success will follow automatically.

You asked me about persistence. Personally, I don't want to

hear a guy talking about having to go to his mother-in-law's house for Thanksgiving Day dinner. He tells his mother-in-law he's going elk hunting and will try to be back in time to have a late dinner with the family. And I don't want to hear about having to go to Great Falls to get a part for the pick-up. A buddy's pick-up can be borrowed to go elk hunting while someone else can go get the part.

Sometimes I don't like myself because I get so adamant about what has to be done to take elk, but those are the facts. Hunters that consistently take elk have a similar attitude. Ninety percent of the successful elk hunters are the same 90 percent that harvest elk year after year.

Question: That's all well and good, but how do you balance a job, family needs, and other responsiblities against taking 14 consecutive days for elk hunting?

Burk: There are certain priorities in my life that have been severely tested through the fires of 17 years of marriage and 42 years of living. I by no means have all the answers, but in my life hunting — particularly elk hunting — is a top priority. The season is short and only rolls around once a year. Hunting has been a very stabilizing and positive influence on my life. Over the years, hunting has helped me immensely to be a complete human being.

It is vital to have a wife who understands the hunting philosophy. She doesn't necessarily have to hunt herself, but she must have an appreciation and tolerance of a husband who does. Had that not been the case in my personal life, my marriage wouldn't have survived very long. There are many women, even though they may be great people, that I would be mentally incompatible with.

Now if my dedication to hunting is such that I totally abuse my wife's and kid's physical and mental needs, I guess I'd better be a bachelor and put hunting as my number one priority. Fortunately for my family and me, I made my feelings concerning hunting crystal-clear before my wife and I tied the knot. Therefore, we have no problems when it comes to hunting.

Let me ask you this: What other activity do you know that brings mental contentment, good physical health, puts food on the table and, as a bonus, when successful, massages one's ego. I can't think of any. I could spend the time taking a vacation in Florida, bitching all the way going and coming and not get the forementioned benefits. Let me go to the proverbial bottom line. If I didn't go hunting, I would be an unhappy person. Therefore, my wife and kids would be unhappy and my job would suffer.

If winter conditions are severe and prolonged, elk can become a problem for ranchers.

Question: What do you think about the future of elk hunting in the Northern Rockies in general and trophy hunting in particular.

Burk: I feel there will be trophy bulls around as long as there is elk hunting, but the opportunity to take a trophy will become more and more limited. Hunting pressure and refinement of hunting techniques by a larger number of elk hunters will continue to affect trophy hunting in an adverse manner.

For instance, when I started seriously bugling and archery hunting elk in the mid-1970s, it was uncommon to have a lot of competition. Now, nearly every outdoor magazine carries one or two articles a year describing how to bugle elk, and the hunting catalogs are offering instructional bugle tapes. All this results in more mature bulls being harvested.

I think we are going to see elk hunting go on a permit basis relatively soon, probably within the next 10 years. The general concept of permit hunting is a poor one. Everyone should get an equal opportunity to hunt by issuing unlimited permits, but only have a certain number of elk come from a given area. The luck of the draw in this situation will not keep a person from hunting. This is how Bighorn sheep are hunted in some areas in Montana today. Strict penalties for not checking harvested elk would keep this type of system viable and policable. Heavy fines and revoking of hunting privileges would insure that people would accept and honor the management criteria.

A cow and calf elk during the summer rearing season.

The Future of Elk Hunting

Elk have been and continue to be a significant part of the American West. No factions clamor for their elimination, as is the case with the grizzly. However, society's resolve and commitment to maintaining a sound and productive elk population is being tested. Current elk populations apparently are stable with no major population changes foreseeable in the near future.

Habitat availability remains the principal factor limiting herd numbers since most ranges in the Northern Rockies now are near or at maximum carrying capacity. High quality winter range is needed most critically. Unfortunately, elk and man begin to rub elbows in that segment of the elk's range. Man covets the low, grassy, south-facing slopes that are also needed by elk in the winter.

Good portions of the elk's winter range   on private land. State fish and game departments, for a number of years, have been purchasing some of these lands to keep them from being developed. However, acquisition is limited by landowner cooperation and the availability of funds.

Since elk inhabit and traverse state and federal lands, cooperation between agencies also is an important aspect of elk management and will have an impact on the future of the herds. In the 1970s, more than 23 percent of elk habitat in the national forests was subject to logging. In the past, the practice was to log first and worry later about the damage done to elk habitat. The reasons were a powerful timber lobby, public apathy, and lack of

Clearcut logging operations, if not done properly, can have a devastating effect on elk habitat.

funds at the state and federal level to study the effects logging activities would have on elk. Recently, interest and activity have increased to identify problems brought about by accelerated, intense logging practices. Of particular concern is the proliferation of logging roads that provide easy access by humans to elk populations and habitat. Research shows that total, periodic or seasonal road closures greatly benefit the elk.

Large areas of designated wilderness have been set aside in the Northern Rockies and since logging and development are not allowed in these areas, they become a sanctuary of sorts. However, uncontrolled use of lands adjacent to wilderness areas can detract from the benefits of these retreats. Winter migration patterns annually force the animals out of the rugged highlands of the legally protected areas and onto the neighboring lands where development is not controlled. Conflicts between game and livestock interests are inevitable in these situations.

Visitors to wilderness areas also are impacting elk populations. Because these public lands encompass some of the most spectacular scenery in the nation, thousands of hikers, campers and hunters visit these remote areas each year. Sheer numbers of people, as well as abuses by some members of these groups, sometimes makes it difficult for the elk to find sanctuary from man.

Management agencies should consider public opinion when

making decisions that affect the future of elk and their habitats. This is especially true when they are dealing with a highly-valued species like elk. One means of doing this is proper application of the Pittman-Robertson funds. In 1936 Congress established that state fish and game agencies receive money collected from an 11 percent tax on sporting arms and ammunition. This money is to be spent on wildlife restoration and management and it is largely because of these funds that elk populations have rebounded to present levels.

In order to qualify for funds, a state had to pledge all hunting and fishing license fees to conservation purposes. Before the law was enacted, much of the money collected from the sale of licenses went to fund highways and other public works project.

Another major benefit of the P-R funds is that many of animals produced from its programs are ultimately harvested by hunters. This is as it should be.

In the future, customary methods of financing various research programs and the purchase of habitat may need to be adjusted. Because of increasing concern for the protection of nongame species, resource management agencies are beginning to shift emphasis away from protecting only game species to protecting popular nongame animals as well. This causes the available funds to be spread even thinner and some states are now contemplating innovative ways to provide additional funds to cope with changing ideals and more complex management problems. These problems will worsen as the nation's lands become more populated.

The amount of acreage holding huntable populations of elk is expected to remain about the same in the immediate future. Exceptions are to be expected, however, in states where changes in land use procedures have decreased the amount of land available to hunters. Some of the reasons are subdivision development on private lands, closure of private lands previously open to hunting, and changes in timber harvest practices. In 1975, the last date for which figures are available, closing of private lands in Montana, for example, reduced the statewide elk harvest by an estimated 3 percent.

As demographics and land use practices continue to change, the characteristics of hunting will change too. Until recently, in Montana for example, general seasons in which either sex elk could be harvested during the first part of the season were held. This has now changed to a cow-by-permit-only method during the general season and even that process is tightening up. The state's general season also was shortened by two days in 1983.

Now hunters in Montana face what their comrades in the other major elk hunting states had already experienced — the likelihood of the general hunting season being reduced to permit-only hunting. Regulations everywhere appear to be slowly getting tighter and tighter as the issues of multiple land-use become more pressing. Improved access to forested areas, increased numbers of hunters willing to penetrate into previously inaccessible back country, and declining elk populations in some hunting districts are other reasons for the trend toward more strict regulations. Illegal kills, plus animals lost due to crippling during the legal hunting periods also must be taken into count. Even with more restrictive regulations, the elk harvest is expected to remain stable since more hunters are afield.

A conflict is growing in some states between resident and nonresident hunters, too. For a variety of reasons resident hunters have criticized the nonresident hunter. As a result, the nonresident has seen a limit on the numbers of licenses issued and a dramatic increase in license fees. Recently a lawsuit was brought against the Montana Department of Fish, Wildlife and Parks because a nonresident hunter thought the fee for a big game hunting license was disproportionately higher than the resident fee. He lost the case. At the same time, resident permits were also increased in the face of extreme resistance.

What will the long-term elk population trends and elk hunting opportunities be in the Northern Rockies? The answer lies within each of us, you and me and our fellow hunters. Can we as individuals conduct our lives and industries within the framework recommended by researchers and game biologists? Will game managers be able to satisfy the needs of the various industries that depend on natural resource development, while at the same time maintaining quality elk habitat? These and other problems promise to be with us for some time yet. The conflict between land use and elk will continue and perhaps become more acute as our country's population increases.

The decisions that will determine which way we go regarding these questions are being made right now and hunters must defend the opportunity to hear the thrilling bugle of a herd bull echoing off the timbered slopes of a remote basin. It's something I think must be considered every American's birthright! The challenge of the future is to give elk and their habitat due consideration wherever and whenever needed, whether they're pressured by the hunter, logging activity, developer, mining industry or the recreationist.

FINAL THOUGHTS, THE PERSONAL DIMENSION

Every September for the past few years I've faced a a terrible, soul-searching dilemma. Football season and the elk rutting season occur simultaneously and my son has been a participant in a local program for young players. And so have I, as a head coach for the past eight seasons.

Now one of the finest moments of my life occurred in the fall of 1983 when the referee blew his whistle ending our team's final game. It ended a gratifying season for this was the championship game, which we won 6-0 when my quarterbacking son scored the only touchdown. But my dilemma was that the game-ending whistle also signaled the end of the elk rut. Early elk season was over and I'd managed to put in only 5 days of bowhunting for elk.

Life is full of priorities and September is very tough on my emotional stability. In 2   seasons, my son Scott will move to junior high ball and I'll retire from the program, my civic responsibility being satisfied. As my good friend Gene Wensel, author of *Hunting Rutting Whitetails,* says, "There are three priorities in my life: family, work and playtime."

I'm now in the process of taking his theory one step farther. Why not combine work and playtime and eliminate the work headache? What if I could make a living doing what gives me a great deal of personal satisfaction, without which my life would be useless. If this could be done, I suspect work would not be work at all.

Obviously hunting and photographing big game are high priorities in my life. But I have asked myself, "Why do I hunt? Why do I enjoy wild animals so much?"

Stoney Burk had the right idea. "Hunting makes me a complete person," he said. "The outdoors gives me an emotional anchor, a solid reference point in the order of my life."

Honestly, there also is an ego factor for me. Hunting elk and big, mountain muley bucks massages my ego plenty simply because of the type of country they live in. We all need that sort of challenge once in a while. To travel light and hunt the remote basins alone or with a close, like-minded friend is the ultimate. I pity the poor roadhunter; he is missing the whole point. I also get satisfaction from returning with a load of meat for my family — must be the Neanderthal in me.

Most hunters come to realize there are several stages of maturation when it comes to hunting. Beginners of any age get heart palpitations at seeing an elk or deer. But as the seasons roll along, does, cows and forkhorns become very acceptable trophies. Success is measured differently at different times in the hunter's life. For some this happens suddenly, while for others it occurs slowly over several seasons. The key is that for most of us it does happen. We discover the ability to pass over does or small bulls. It is a good feeling to have an animal in your sights, a sure kill, and pass it by. That is the final stage of the hunter's maturity, to hold out for a superior animal. And as Rob Hazlewood says, "I like to extend my season as long as possible."

In addition, I've wrestled with a great paradox in my life. Likely you have too. I'm a veterinarian, so much of my work involves saving animals' lives. Some anti-hunters have asked me, "How can you profess to love and respect animals, and then kill them?" It is a provocative, legitimate question — one not easily answered. Why do I nurse a fawn that has been hit by a car back to health? Why do we risk bruises and contusions to untangle a struggling doe from a fence? And taking the question farther, why are hunters the first in line with funds and volunteer work to rescue a herd of winter-starved elk?

A hard look at the facts makes it apparent that man is the only contemporary predator capable of controlling herd sizes. If animal populations are not kept in balance with the habitat, mass starvation occurs — and a starving elk is not a pretty sight. It is a slow, painful death and the other side of the story is that the habitat suffers badly too from overuse and takes years to restore itself so it can support viable game populations. Hunting is pure and simple a management tool for the betterment and perpetuation of a species, and I want very much to leave a healthy wildlife legacy to my kids or, for that matter, to all kids in America.

Other justifications for taking game are cloudy and less defined. For example, other considerations are satisfying a primitive instinctive urge (man has been a hunter for hundreds of thousands of years), bringing home food, and the gratification earned from pitting inferior eyes and ears but a superior brain against those of a wild animal.

Sure, I feel a twinge of remorse as I bury my face in a bull elk's hide, look into his still eyes, and feel the texture of his antlers. But deep inside, I realize this is the order of things and all is good. Elk have been and will continue to be a part of the American West, and my life. But the degree to which they will remain a major part of our outdoor heritage is very much in doubt. Our resolve and commitment to maintaining sound, productive elk herds is being tested. The elk's future will depend on finding the delicate balance between the needs of all segments of society now making demands on the country's natural resources, and my guess is that it's going to be the elk hunters who end up being the elk's best friend. The answer to this major problem, really, lies within each one of us.